Janice Lynne Lundy is a wonderful writer with deep understanding, and it felt quite amazing to be reflected in her eyes. Her careful listening and clear seeing is a grace.

Joan Borysenko, PhD
Author of *A Woman's Journey to God* and
Inner Peace for Busy Women

Women need to be reassured of their worth and of the immense possibilities of their own spiritual growth. We cannot emphasize often enough the "ordinariness" of holiness and also its profoundness and enormous possibilities. This is done very well in *Your Truest Self*. Janice Lynne Lundy offers an excellent resource for women. Her style and approach are just what women today are longing for. The message, and Jan's intimate connection to the reader, come together in an excellent, inspiring, and informative way. I sense this book will give women great courage.

Joyce Rupp
Author of *Praying Our Goodbyes* and *Open the Door*

If there's any thing women need today, it's a sense of their own value—not in the workplace or behind a mop, but through an awareness of their spiritual essence. We need to know that who we are is precious, what we have is needed, and that we are leading the way for all humanity. Through the shining example of the extraordinary women in *Your Truest Self*, we can all be inspired to move a little farther down our path as women of grace and strength.

Daphne Rose Kingma
Author of *Loving Yourself*

Self-realization can be misunderstood as selfish and self-centered but, in fact, it is exactly the opposite. Realizing who we truly are and gently encouraging ourselves to live an authentic life is vitally important for us and for the good of the world as a whole. Jan Lundy's wisdom and love shine through *Your Truest Self* and are invaluable guides for readers who long to become aware of and embrace the strong, compassionate, and creative women they are at the heart of their being. Finding and expressing your true self is the most precious and joyous gift you can give to yourself and others.

Sue Patton Thoele
Author of *The Courage To Be Yourself, The Woman's Book of Courage,* and *The Mindful Woman*

Jan Lundy invites all women to see themselves as "holy women" by virtue of their very existence. She shares her own spiritual transformation by focusing on a dozen well-known mentors whose spiritual journeys inspired her own. Finally, she offers practical and powerful ways to discover a "sacred space within ourselves" where we can create an authentic connection with Spirit.

Maril Crabtree
Author of *Sacred Waters: Stories of Healing, Cleansing, and Renewal*

Janice Lynne Lundy's inspirational book overflows with spiritual wisdom. She entices us on a journey to reclaim ourselves as holy women and provides us with the perfect companions—twelve bold, courageous women whose shining light provides the perfect navigation on our search for spiritual meaning.

Karen Ely
Author of *Daring to Dream* and *A Retreat of My Own*
Founder of A Woman's Way Retreats, Sedona, Arizona

Jan Lundy has drawn together the thoughts and wisdom of admirable, transparent women. The words, the wisdom, the practical suggestions, and Jan's own honest narrative are a glowing blueprint for wholeness. You will not read *Your Truest Self* quickly; you will stop again and again to integrate the knowledge and to respond from the place of your own deepest knowing.

Paula D'Arcy
Author of *Gift of the Red Bird*

What a beautifully written, inspiring book! It softly, yet powerfully, conveys the joy of discovering—and valuing—our true spiritual essence. The journey to know ourselves at our core requires great courage. Yet, with incredibly wise, holy women like Jan Lundy and those she interviewed guiding the way, the path is much easier. This book will give every woman hope and clarity for finding greater peace.

Megan Raphael
Author of *The Courage Code*

Janice Lynne Lundy's precious book came at a critical time when I was searching for a deeper meaning to my life . . . searching for "me." While there are many golden nuggets to be found inside, the passage that resonated with me the most is found right in the introduction: "Study and training do not bring any of us home to our truest selves. Living does." *Your Truest Self* is the perfect antidote for a bruised heart, a yearning soul, and a genuine healing of the mind.

Nancy Vogl
Co-editor of *Chicken Soup for the Single Parent's Soul* and co-author of *Am I a Color Too?*

Jan Lundy's prayerfully collected interviews with twelve deeply spiritual women provide the framework for *Your Truest Self: Embracing the Woman You Are Meant To Be*, a meaningful and enriching journey of self-discovery. By wrapping each story around a spiritual truth, Jan illuminates the path to greater acceptance and self-love, while also offering reflections and practical observations based in her own experience. Make time for this book—carefully read these engaging stories, thoughtfully answer the Reflection Questions, and prayerfully sit alone with the meditations at the end of each chapter. Make time, and you will finally begin to hear the holy woman who has been quietly whispering from your soul.

Joni Hubred-Golden
Publisher of the Michigan Women's Forum

If you've ever asked, "Who am I? Why am I here? Where did I come from? Where am I going?" this seminal book by Jan Lundy will assist you in finding answers for yourself. It is a journey into selfhood each woman must initiate on her own. With Jan's inspiring collection of wisdom from authentic Holy Women, including herself, you will not be traveling this transformational journey alone.

Pamela Harman Daugavietis
Editor of *Women's Voices, Women's Visions*

your truest self

Embracing
the Woman
You Are Meant
to Be

Janice Lynne Lundy

SORIN BOOKS  Notre Dame, Indiana

www.sorinbooks.com

ISBN-10 1-933495-12-X   ISBN-13 978-1-933495-12-5

Cover and text design by John R. Carson.

Cover illustration © Nicholas Monu.

Printed and bound in the United States of America.

Library of Congress Cataloging-in-Publication Data

Your truest self : embracing the woman you are meant to be / Janice Lynne Lundy.
        p. cm.
    Includes bibliographical references.
    ISBN-13: 978-1-933495-12-5 (pbk.)
    ISBN-10: 1-933495-12-X (pbk.)
    1. Self-realization in women. 2. Self-acceptance in women. 3. Self-perception in women. 4. Women--Psychology. I. Lundy, Janice Lynne.
    HQ1206.Y73 2008
    155.6'33--dc22

                                                    2008026173

For you, because you are ready
to live by the light of your own truth,
and for my mother, Lorraine,
and my husband, Brad,
whose unconditional love and
support help me to live mine.

Contents

On foot I had to walk through the solar systems,
before I found the first thread of my red dress.

Edith Södergran

A Holy Longing . . .

You are that which you are seeking.

St. Francis of Assisi

For as long as I can remember, I've had a love affair with "holy women." I have put them on pedestals and adored them. I have admired them from afar and, at times, even sat at their feet.

As a young girl, I lived down the street from a Dominican convent and was a voyeur of the black and white–garbed nuns who tended the gardens and grounds. I wondered what went on behind those mysterious, private walls to make them seem, as they did to me, aglow with godliness. As an anthropology student in college, I was drawn to study indigenous medicine women, midwives, and healers—all of whom surely endured long hours of training, self-sacrifice, and service to be designated by their people as "holy." In recent years, my imagination has been captured by mystics, saints, and sages, women who prayed without ceasing and communed with angels.

I came to understand, in fact, that I longed to *be* a holy woman. I ached for the inner peace I saw reflected on their faces, because most days I could not access a glimmer of my own. I coveted the confidence reflected in their bearing and the courage with which they walked through life, for I seemed to stumble again and again when my life's path became rocky. I ached for a faith like theirs that was unshakable, for I was often filled with self-doubt, uncertain what I believed about any number of things, including God. But what I really hungered for, more than any of the qualities these esteemed women represented, was a spiritual life that was real and authentic, one that would nourish and sustain me every day of my life.

I pondered: What does it mean to be a holy woman, and how do you become one? I wondered, how do you live in a sacred manner? Were there certain things a woman must do, choices she must make, to create a Spirit-filled life for herself? And, if so, what would those choices be? Was there a path to follow to become more peaceful, confident, and faithful? I sincerely hoped there was, because I was determined to find it.

For more than three decades, I followed a Spirit trail. I tracked the footsteps of dozens of women of diverse spiritualities whom the Divine seemed to bring into my life at exactly the right time: perhaps through a chance meeting or a professional one, through their writings or creative expressions, or by attending one of their workshops. The trail took me from Protestant Christianity in my twenties; through forays into Buddhism and yoga in my thirties; through the goddess movement,

Sufism, and Native American spirituality in my forties. I made pilgrimages to sacred sites, walked labyrinths, chanted at temples, meditated at ashrams, and danced on moonlit beaches with circles of women. It was a spiritual sampling of grand proportions, and because I was so hungry for a soul-satisfying taste of Spirit, I gobbled up whatever came my way.

Despite all my searching during those wondrous wandering years, this journey did not reveal a spirituality that fit me like a glove, despite what I had hoped. I did realize that by walking it I had become, over time, more peace-filled, because I'd learned the value of silence, the power of meditation; more courageous, because I'd ventured outside of my comfort zone to explore new spiritual horizons; more compassionate, because in my travels, I had seen compassion modeled for me by hundreds of people from all walks of life who were generous and openhearted.

Even though I'd experienced "spiritual" growth in myself, I still did not *feel* spiritual enough. Granted, I'd learned spiritual truths along the way, but I was certain I fell short when it came to applying them. I continued to stumble and fall when life presented challenges, or I closed my heart to others when I experienced hurt or fear. On the spiritual path, I felt more off the track than on. I still longed to be a holy woman, but no matter how far I searched, no matter how hard I tried, I couldn't seem to make that happen. It appeared I was destined to be an ordinary woman living an ordinary life.

I remember the day when my thinking changed. I had just completed a two-year training program to become a spiritual director, a certified spiritual counselor who guides and supports others on their personal journeys.

(In hindsight, I realize even this may have been one more attempt on my part to *feel* holy or be more spiritual.) My teacher, Judy Hahn, a former Dominican sister, wrote me an e-mail, thanking me for a small gift I had given her. The words in her correspondence leapt off the page at me, surprising me with their pronouncement. "You are a holy woman," she wrote, "and I am honored to have walked with you."

My stomach lurched in response to those words. How could she have known my innermost desire—to be a holy woman? I had never spoken of this to her, or to anyone for that matter, so her words shook me to the core. I thought, certainly she must be mistaken. Because my lack of confidence was so profound, I could not absorb her words. Instead, I continued to count the hundreds of ways that I was not fit to walk in the shoes of those honorable women I idealized. I knew the many times I still judged others, held back support, or closed my heart altogether. I was not as peaceful as them, nor as confident. Certainly Judy was mistaken. I was no holy woman.

Yet I also knew that Judy was no fool. She was one of the holiest women I had ever met. She was connected to her spirit and to God. She emanated openheartedness and generosity. She was both humble and self-assured. She was peaceful. What struck me the most about her was that her outer life mirrored her inner life. She lived her spirituality thoroughly. In every conversation or situation that arose, you could feel her spiritual integrity. Judy lived her spiritual truths.

My thoughts swirled riotously, trying to wrap themselves around the idea that someone else actually perceived *me* to be holy. Had I done something special?

Arrived at some level of accomplishment to be recognized as such? When did this occur, and why didn't I feel it happening? The questions spun in succession, and tears of frustration rolled down my cheeks as I continued to stare at Judy's words: "You are a holy woman."

Within moments, through what I can only describe as an act of grace, a sense of calm washed over me. The warm, syrupy feeling, the loving energy that I have come to know today as Mother Mary, enfolded me in invisible arms. I could feel and hear her in the recesses of my heart, that deep, knowing place where truth inevitably triumphs over falsehood. Her voice—or was it my own inner voice?—assured me that what Judy said was true. *I am a holy woman. And so is every other woman who walks this earth.*

Words and images flooded in to show me how I had been holding on to a faulty notion of personal holiness. I realized I had spent my entire life searching outside myself for a divine connection, one that would be accepted and recognized by others. In those life-changing moments, I was given a glimpse into my true identity and into the true identity of all women. We really *are* holy, not because of anything we have done or can ever do, but by the simple nature of our birth. We are holy women because we come from the Divine. We are made of spirit, we have a soul, and in that we are holy from the moment we are born. Holy is what we are in our natural state. Despite all our human frailties, our weaknesses, and our faults, we are holy women. We have been all along. We just don't believe it.

On that fateful day when I accepted the truth of Judy's e-mail, I began to reclaim myself as holy—to live as my truest self. A passion began to simmer in me to access the Sacred One within, to live in a bold, new way, and to help others do the same. I vowed to overcome the voices of self-doubt that had plagued me most of my life, which said I must be or do something special to be considered sacred.

As I looked about me, I began to see more and more women like myself struggling with these very same issues—issues of worth, identity, and personal acceptance. My hope in putting these words on paper is that you will join me on this journey to reclaim yourself as holy and live as your truest self. In fact, it is your birthright and destiny to do so. To once and for all relinquish any fear or insecurity that could prevent you from experiencing personal freedom—spiritual freedom—to live as the woman you are meant to be.

Granted, I have not found this to be an easy task, nor may it be easy for you if you decide to join me, because old habits and outmoded ways of thinking are difficult to cast aside. Thankfully, the journey can be made easier for us if we walk with a trusted companion or two. This book you hold in your hands is filled to overflowing with companions for our journey together. They are some of the holiest women I have come to know, and their coming together in this way provides a path that we can all follow to live glorious, Spirit-filled lives.

They are bold women, courageous women. Altruistic and generous-of-spirit. Visionary. And vulnerable, in that they have chosen to share with you their deepest thoughts, fears, sorrows, and victories as they have learned to live in a sacred manner. Here are women who have struggled to find inner peace, self-confidence, and courage. Due to a burning passion to live from their fullness, no matter what challenges life offers them, they continue to thrive, remaining deeply connected to their spirit and the greater Spirit, God. By sharing their personal journeys with you in this way, they know we will *all* grow and thrive. Together, we can heal from past hurts, conquer our fears, and create miracles in our lives to become the luminous beings we were born to be.

The women you will meet here are writers and teachers, activists and artists. Some are well known; others are not. It is an ecumenical gathering of women from many spiritualities and religious persuasions, seekers and finders all.

As for my personal relationship with them, a few have been faithful mentors, their benevolent spirits and loving words urging me on whenever I'd lose my way. Some I have never met, having only savored their books and spoken with them on the telephone, but their powerful and public holy-woman personas served as bright beacons for navigating my own stormy seas. Others are new friends, and we are finding our way together.

Within these pages, I'll share with you how I have come to know these remarkable women and what their light-filled presence has revealed to me, can reveal to all of us. Allow me to briefly introduce them here in the order you will meet them in this book.

> **Joyce Rupp**—An author, retreat leader, and member of the Servants of Mary community, who encourages us to create a woman-friendly spirituality for ourselves.
>
> **Jan Phillips**—A photographer, writer, and modern-day mystic, who invites us to

get reacquainted with our body and its wisdom to better experience the Sacred.

Iyanla Vanzant—A best-selling author and spiritual life coach who empowers us to choose thoughts and emotions that lead us into the Spirit.

Dudley Evenson—A musician and cofounder of Soundings of the Planet, a record label promoting personal and planetary peace through music, who demonstrates how to create daily spiritual practices that connect us with the Divine One within.

Sue Patton Thoele—A psychotherapist and celebrated author of self-help and spiritual-growth books for women, who invites us to live gently with ourselves by tending our self and spirit.

Daphne Rose Kingma—An author and psychotherapist, whose life's mission is to teach us how to love so that we might see the Divine in everything and everyone.

Doreen Virtue, PhD—An author and workshop facilitator, fondly dubbed "The Angel Lady," who can help us connect with the higher realms, opening ourselves to the power of grace.

Michelle Tsosie Sisneros—An award-winning Native American artist and illustrator living a traditional life at Santa Clara Pueblo, who shows us how to start over and cocreate each day anew with the help of the Spirit.

Naomi Judd—A country music singer, author, and talk show host, a passionate proponent of mind, body, spirit medicine who personifies how adversity and Dark Nights of the Soul bring us to greater healing.

Juan Borysenko, PhD—A mind/body scientist, author, and lecturer who affirms that each of us journeys into the Divine in our own, unique way and in our own special timing.

Frances Moore Lappé—An author and cofounder of two activist organizations whose efforts inspire us to overcome fear and harness the courage to speak and live our truths independent of the opinions of others.

Mari Gayatri Stein—An illustrator, author, and yoga and meditation teacher who demonstrates compassion and unconditional love for self and others so that we might live as brothers and sisters in oneness.

Within these pages you will discover twelve Transformational Truths, distilled from my encounters with
these women. Each truth is a spiritual principle to live
by if you desire to live as your truest self. You will find
that these truths will help you embrace your sacred self,
enabling you to live a full, rich-in-Spirit life characterized by inner peace, joy, and great purpose, just like the
women featured in this book.

At the end of each chapter, you will find Reflection
Questions and a Peaceful Pause. Both are opportunities
to quiet yourself and reflect upon the truth that has
been presented. Taking time for personal reflection,
done inwardly or through journaling, will enable you
to clearly assess your current capacity to embody that
particular truth. A "peaceful pause" is a time to put
your mind at ease, breathe, and remember your divine
connection. Each pause will provide you with moments
of peaceful interlude, an occasion to spend precious time
with your sacred self, and deeply listen to the movement
of the Spirit within you.

I have learned so much from spending time with each
of these spiritual mentors. As you'll discover, the women
featured in this book are not "holier than thou" or meant
to be placed on pedestals and revered. They are real
women, women like you and me, who still on occasion
struggle with their notions of personal holiness in light
of the times in which we live.

A universal call has been sounded to live in an
enlightened new way, and the women featured here
beckon us to answer. They demonstrate, by the very
model of their lives, that no matter what culture or religious background we come from, affirming our innate
holiness and embracing it is at the core of our spiritual

journeys. When we profess our desire to live in a sacred manner, to be more peaceful, openhearted, trusting, faithful, and generous, our journey deepens, bringing about profound healing. When we recognize that we are daughters of the universe, made of spirit and stardust, our lives will become sanctified, made holy and whole once again.

I've written this book not because I have arrived at this place myself, but because, like any of us, my life is a work in progress. I continue to reclaim my truest self more and more each day. Even though I am a trained teacher of comparative religions, a spiritual director and mentor, and an associate of a religious order, I now know that these vocations do not ensure connection with my sacred self. Study and training do not bring any of us home to our truest selves. Living does.

In the words of Abraham Joshua Heschel, "Just to be is a blessing. Just to live is holy." I have learned that it is in our living and being that holiness arrives, not upon the wings of a great wind, but within the gentle breath of life that moves through us. We need do nothing special to call ourselves holy women, only take a first step, no matter whether it be sturdy or faltering, toward our truest selves. It is our life's purpose to embrace the totality of who we are—wholeness—pure and simple. For "holiness" and "wholeness" come from the same root word, have the same origin, and to accept one is to gain the other. When we acknowledge our sacred source, we will begin to recognize ourselves as the glorious women we are and embark on the ultimate journey toward feeling holy and whole once again. My desire is for this book to assist you in that process.

Hildegard of Bingen, the great twelfth-century German abbess, affirmed, "At birth our divine potential is folded up in us like a tent. It is life's purpose to unfold that tent." I believe Hildegard is right, her sentiment echoing a message that could not be more seasonable, considering the challenging times in which we live. It *is* time to remember our divine origin and potential, time to live from our fullness and fill the world with the light from our radiance. May we join hands and hearts and live as our truest selves. For when we do, the world will never be the same . . .

How to Use This Book

Before you begin the journey through the pages of this book, I'd like to offer a few suggestions for how to proceed.

Though each chapter focuses on one particular mentor and it would seem natural to pick and choose whom you might enjoy reading about first, please start at the beginning. This book and its chapters unfold in a purposeful way, in a specific order, from simple to complex, especially as far as integrating the Transformational Truths are concerned.

This book is a spiritual-journey book, a trek inward, with a stepping-off place and a hoped-for destination, and you are the pilgrim. By moving through the chapters intentionally, savoring their revelations and taking time to reflect upon them, you will begin to unravel old ways of thinking and embrace exciting, new ways of being. Learning to live in a new way takes time. Therefore, this is a not a book to be read in one sitting or even in a few. My greatest hope is that it will become your companion, a trustworthy guide for going deeper, one small step at a time.

Each chapter will invite you to personally reflect upon its Transformational Truth in two ways. The first is through the Reflection Questions. I encourage you to take the time to answer these questions. If you engage in the practice of journaling, write down your answers and any thoughts that emerge. Give voice to your hesitations, fears, hopes, and dreams. Record your successes. If you are not an active journaler, you may want to challenge yourself to be. Journaling is quite enjoyable, even fun, as well as healing, empowering, and transformative. If we avoid taking the time to reflect upon our experiences, we will continue to engage in the same patterns of thinking and being that we always have. Reflection through journaling can usher in the clarity we need to make important life changes—changes that will bring us into greater alignment with our truest selves and the Divine.

The second way to reflect upon each Transformational Truth is to use the Peaceful Pause found at the end of each chapter. Most of us are in the habit of rush-reading through books to get to where we think we need to go— toward the end—to be done. Where we need to go within this book is not toward the end, but into the middle, deep down inside ourselves, into the quiet place within where our spirit resides. A Peaceful Pause is one vehicle that can take us there. Hurrying on to the next chapter, hoping for the next brilliant awareness breakthrough, will not help us embody our truest selves. Sitting quietly, alone with ourselves, at home in our sacred center where peace and love naturally abide, will.

Each Peaceful Pause is intended to help you slow down, so give yourself time to do just that. Before you begin, take time to shake off the world. Take as much time as you need to settle down into your body, slowing down the activity of your mind. By bringing your attention to your in-breath and your out-breath, you can facilitate this process. Read the entire pause through first (some have very specific purposes—release of fear, for example, or opening up your heart); then proceed.

Use the pauses as often as you can, anytime you wish. In the busyness of our days, we all need precious moments of time when there is nothing else we need do but *be*; to become quiet; to be still and know; to enter that very special place within our own being where our spirit can commune with the Greater Spirit, the God in whom we are sourced, sustained, and enlivened.

May your journey be fruitful and blessed!

My True Identity
Is Spirit

Before the end of my journey may I reach within myself
the One which is the All.

Rabindranath Tagore

Without trumpets or fanfare she found me again, this woman whom I have come to adore. She appeared on a blustery winter day as I strolled the aisles of my local bookstore. Her image appeared to rise up from the cover of a brown spiral-bound journal, a levitating mirage. Palms open, arms out to the side, she looked like Jennifer Jones in the movie *The Song of Bernadette*, her serene face gently framed within a flowing white head covering. As the image descended, reclaiming its place on the journal, I noticed a line of subtle gold text written on the cover, inviting me to take a closer look: "Confess," it read.

The word set me back a pace, for these were not the loving words I had come to associate with the Blessed Mother Mary. I have only experienced her over the years as unconditionally loving and comforting. Here she was issuing a directive, strong and compelling, ordering me to do something with which I was completely unfamiliar.

Confess? Confess what? Had I done something wrong? Why was Mary beseeching me to admit things?

1

And what things? I was not traditionally religious and, truthfully, a directive such as this raised my hackles, reminding me of daunting stories I'd heard from friends of visits to dark church confessionals to admit their "sins" to the parish priest. Certainly Mary was not asking this of me. Or was she?

Despite my discomfort, I picked up the journal and looked inside. It was completely blank, except for the first page, which said:

> Confess unto me
> your innermost thoughts,
> your deepest desires,
> your darkest secrets,
> your most desperate longings.
> For, I shall not judge thee,
> but embrace thee.[1]

Immediately, an intense wave of warmth cascaded over me and tears came. The words on the page rang true. Yes, I had shared my deepest thoughts, desires and fears with her, the light and the dark of me. And when I had, she had not abandoned or judged me. She embraced, welcomed me into her luxurious lap of love like a devoted parent would, just as she has done for millions of others worldwide who have called upon her time and again for help or comfort.

What remained confusing, however, was this suggestion to confess. I truly did not know what she meant. Trusting in time that I would understand this request, I purchased the journal anyway, took it home, and placed it on my nightstand. As the days passed, I remained puzzled. What *was* this holy woman asking of me?

~~~

If you are passionate about living as your truest self, there will come a time when you will have to discern what it is you really believe—to confess, as I have come to understand it now—to say what you know. Two months had gone by before I realized this was exactly what Mother Mary was urging me to do that day in the bookstore: to be clear about who I was, to speak honestly about what I believed. She was asking me if I was ready to live my truths publicly for all the world to see.

As our journeys unfold, each of us will need to determine what it is we have come to know as personal truth. "Know thyself," Socrates said, for self-knowledge will lead to God-knowledge. "Tell me your beliefs, and I will tell you who you are," said another, unknown philosopher, indicating that our beliefs form the basis of how we choose to live. To walk in the world as our truest selves we must first uncover the core beliefs that form the basis of our thoughts, feelings, and actions, whether they be lofty or base, original or borrowed, true or false for us.

And so I pose this same question to you that I have posed to myself many times over the years: *Who are you, and what do you really believe?*

Do you believe that you are a spiritual being, a sacred and holy woman? Or do you believe that you are a tragically flawed human who must strive for acceptance, perfection? Are you perhaps unsure of what you believe at all? No matter what answer comes, rest assured it is the perfect one for you for now. It affirms who you think you are in this moment and, in the eyes of the Divine One, you are perfect just the way you are. There are no correct answers here, no guilt, no shame. Even if you perceive yourself to be lost or disconnected, it is still the right place to be—for now. If you are committed to connecting more deeply with your spiritual self, by answering this simple question and remaining open to new possibilities, you will deepen in self-awareness, allowing your truest self to emerge.

I understand that the precept I propose here—that we are spiritual beings—may be difficult to understand because, in all likelihood, it is not a notion with which we have been raised. To consider ourselves as such was not the language of self we were taught to speak as children. Our beliefs about our true nature have been formulated, shaped, and misshaped by our families and communities, our institutions and their mores, for so long now that it is difficult to discern who we are in our truest form. It is only through going deep within ourselves and carefully listening to the voice of the spirit that resides there, instead of the voices outside of ourselves, that we are able to reconnect with our divine nature.

If we doubt this to be true, it may also be because we have not allowed ourselves to spend time with our innermost, sacred self. In fact, we may not even know who that self is. We may have had brief glimpses of our divine connection, but they remain just that, fleeting moments of spiritual awareness. We may have had a few "ah ha" experiences, passing feelings of inner peace, or a temporary sense of great oneness with and love for others. These occasions don't last, for it seems that within seconds, our human, rational mind jumps in to tell us that this is extraordinary and uncommon to our way of being. Times like these are "special," not part of everyday existence. They are not "real."

In reality, they are not glimpses into "another world," but insights into our very nature. If we are of Spirit, of course we will have "spiritual" experiences that support that connection. It is only our human, ego self that frames it differently and tells us that spiritual experience is outside of ourselves, or is accessible only intermittently. This human ego self coerces us into faulty thinking that perpetuates the belief that perhaps only "special" or "gifted" people have access to the Divine.

This same principle applies to our understanding of what we must do to possess the spiritual qualities we so often hear attributed to wisdom-bearing others. We believe that we must, for example, *strive* for inner peace, that peace exists outside ourselves, a lofty and elusive "spiritual" quality to be sought after or grappled with. This is more faulty human thinking. In reality, if we do have feelings of peacefulness, though sporadic, it means we *do* have peace at our core. It is our God-imbued nature to be peaceful and to live harmoniously with ourselves and others. Such peacefulness only needs to be recognized, accessed, and brought to the surface of our being on a daily basis. The same is true of love, compassion, generosity, patience, or gratitude—any qualities we have deemed spiritual in nature. They reside within all of us. They are sourced in our true nature—Spirit.

This is not a new message. In fact, it is very ancient. From Hindu yogis to Buddhist avatars, from Christian mystics to Sufi poets, the message has been there all along: You and the Divine are one. The ultimate goal of all religions and spiritualities is union with the Divine. According to Cistercian monk Thomas Keating, "To be on the journey to Divine union is really the greatest contribution we can make to the human family."[2] By whatever name we know it in our tradition—God, Love, Jehovah, Allah, Brahma, the All—our purpose here on earth is to rediscover our connection with it and live in accordance with its truths. Those truths bring us to the places we have been longing for our entire lives—vistas of inner peace, harmony, love, abundance, and so much more. They dwell within us, having been there from the moment of our birth.

For those of us who long to join our truest selves with the Spirit in a more authentic way than we have previously, we must begin to accept ourselves as the daughters of the Divine that we are. For many women, as was the case with me, belief may not be enough. Even though we may intellectually understand the concepts I have shared here, it does not mean we will internalize them. And, if we are candid, on any given day we probably do not "feel" like we are holy. I've had to ask myself this many times: If I know what I believe, why do I not *feel* like I am of Spirit? For a myriad of reasons we postpone reclaiming ourselves as spiritual beings. Nor do we live from that perspective. Why does this continue to happen, and why is embracing our true nature such a difficult task for us?

The answer may be amazingly simple—our ego likes it that way. Our ego has been deciding for us since the moment we were born what we needed and desired. The human ego I refer to is not our egotistical self, our self-centeredness, or our inflated self-image (though it may be evidenced as that). It is the amazing mental/emotional system within our human self that is programmed to keep us safe and secure. Father Thomas Keating appropriately refers to it as our "false self," the self developed in our human likeness rather than in the likeness of God.[3] This false self—our ego self—is the self-image developed to cope with the emotional trauma of early childhood. It seeks happiness through satisfying our survival-based needs—security, affection, esteem, control, power. This false self bases its self-worth on cultural or group identification. It keeps us rooted in fear and insecurity. Our ego, operating in this way, keeps us separated from our true nature—our spiritual self.

The ego is not bad, as some would propose, just rooted in base emotions that keep us embroiled in inner turmoil and in conflict with others, immersed in feelings that do not support the highest qualities of our true spiritual nature: peace, love, and joy. Our task in reclaiming ourselves as spiritual beings is to listen less and less to the cries of our ego and its negative thoughts and emotions.

In *Daily Meditations for Practicing the Course,* author Karen Casey describes the ego as a "problem child" who likes to get its way. She writes, "Let us not be ashamed of having an ego. We all have one. Jesus had one too. It's the ease with which we relinquish our ego-driven responses that reveals how much more divine than human we are."[4]

I propose that it is the ego that keeps us from believing and feeling like we are holy women. Depending on our family upbringing and the culture in which we live, the ego speaks to each of us differently. As an American woman, the relentless ego voice I listened to over the years tried to convince me that I was "not enough." I had to be more, do more; I was not all right as I was. Ideals of perfection always twinkled on the horizon, beckoning me closer, falsely guaranteeing me self-satisfaction, personal happiness, and acceptance.

I also realized that this disaffirming, self-doubting ego voice had been joined by the voices of thousands of others over time, within my culture, from one institution to the next, who told me, who tell all women, that we are "less than," thereby keeping us powerless and controllable. In America, this collective voice is heard most prominently through the media, which promote a message that women need to be smarter, thinner, richer, sexier; must be Superwomen capable of taking care of everything and everyone. Magazine headlines, billboards, and television commercials bombard us with messages that we are sorely lacking; then they show us what we need, must buy, or do to be accepted by others. Our religious institutions do the same when they espouse doctrine that encourages us to be more devout, pure, chaste, humble, and self-effacing to be acceptable to God. They encourage us to strive for earthly perfection, reminding us there will ultimately come a day when we'll be judged on how well we mastered those virtues.

Time and again, in more ways than I can count, my own ego voice joined this cacophony of ego voices, reinforcing any insecurity and self-doubt I harbored. This voice kept me small and tied by sturdy apron strings to someone else's opinions and standards. It also kept me afraid to claim a grander version of myself. This is a voice we all have within us, and if it speaks loudly enough, over the years we actually begin to believe what it says. We must be and do certain things to be accepted, to be loved.

It is also a vocalization, often sourced in our families, communities, churches, and temples, which urges us not to question the beliefs and values commonly held by the group, precepts that ensure its survival and status quo. These voices tell us not to think or act differently, not to challenge established truth, even if it might, perchance, be based in falsehood. Don't rock the boat; don't think outside the box; don't ask, period.

In her book *Called to Question: A Spiritual Memoir,* Joan Chittister, O.S.B., offers us a compelling example of someone who publicly confesses to questioning all the dictates that have been handed down to her from one institution to the next, from family, to church, to the greater society throughout her lifetime. She addresses well what many of us ponder with trepidation and fear. Do we dare question all that we have been told until now? Do we risk the displeasure of others to live from our highest nature? Sr. Joan poses the question that burns in all of us if we are bold enough to ask it: "Is openness to other ideas infidelity or is it the beginning of spiritual maturity?"[5]

To live as our truest selves, we must "grow up" spiritually. We must question and then remain open to what truths emerge in response. However, the very act of questioning is difficult for many of us, for it is yet one more arena where the ego can come out to play. To question, to sift and sort through all the emotion-filled, judgment-laden possibilities available to us can feel like an ominous task, and risky. At least that is how our ego would have us perceive it. We have the choice, however, to frame it differently. To question and decipher answers independent of others is an act of freedom. When we give ourselves permission to explore, to experiment, to listen for the unique way the Divine is speaking to us, we grow up spiritually.

All the great ones have questioned—our scientists and theologians, our leaders and teachers, and, most especially, the mystics: men and women who have experienced the Divine in unconventional ways—ways that did not fit the mold of the day. By having the great courage to challenge set norms, the mystics broke that mold and either changed the institution itself or embarked on a bold, new life path. This is the nature of the holy woman's journey: to question, to discern, to cast off what no longer works and supply our own answers. This allows us to don new garb for the journey into our truest selves in God.

My favorite "coming to spiritual maturity" story features St. Teresa of Avila. A sixteenth-century Carmelite nun from Spain, St. Teresa believed that the Divine dwelled within each of us. She knew this, not because she was taught it, as that was not the theology of the times, but because she experienced it firsthand. For years, she was gifted with ecstatic visions in which she conversed with God, who revealed great insights for our spiritual journeys. Relating these to Church clerics brought disdain. In fact, they directed her to stop having them and judged her visionary experiences as sourced in Satan. Despite their earthly mandate, Teresa's visions continued, resulting in her authoring the great spiritual classic *The Interior Castle*.

Throughout Teresa's life, writes Megan Don, author of *Falling into the Arms of God: Meditations with Teresa of Avila*, "she encountered numerous objections and hostilities, both from within and outside the order, and was thrown into fear and self-doubt. Teresa battled with this self-doubt for many years, but with continued faith in her inner God-self, she fought long and hard against

the many male clerics who ceaselessly tried to invalidate
her spiritual experiences. Through this she became an
advocate for self-guidance."[6]

We honor Teresa's spirit when we question, listen
deeply for what rings true for us, choose the voice that
validates our sacred self, and then live accordingly,
making those truths manifest in the world. She serves as
a bright beacon we can look toward when the personal
and collective voice of self-doubt begs to be heard. Teresa
heard what the naysayers proclaimed, but she did not
listen. Nor do we have to.

Like Teresa, I believed with every ounce of my being
that I was, indeed, a spiritual being. However, the process of writing this book brought me to the realization
that despite a lifelong passion for spiritual truth, years
of exploration and study, and even serving as a teacher,
spiritual director, and mentor, I was still tuning in to a
niggling inner voice that kept me unfaithful to my truest
self. Granted, it was certainly more quiet than in the
past, but it was still vocal enough to cast large shadows
of doubt on my ability to speak and live my truth as I
perceived it, much less to write a book on the subject.
In particular, who was I to write to other women about
accessing their holy woman selves when I have had
difficulty accessing my own?

In looking back on the incident in the bookstore that
day, I can now see how the call to "confess" written on
the journal's cover was to serve as the catalyst for hon-
ing in on any remnants of my own self-doubt that still
lurked in the shadows. Discovering the journal was an
act of grace, a very personal invitation from the Spirit to
pay attention, to let go, and to move on. It was time to
grow up and into my truest self. Opportunities like this

come to all of us, but we don't always notice them. We are consistently beckoned by the Spirit to release beliefs and thought patterns that no longer support who we truly are and who we are becoming. We are simply not listening, watching, or attentively faithful to these acts of grace that masquerade as everyday, ordinary events— like a journal lying on a sale table in a bookstore.

The first step toward welcoming graces such as this into our lives is to acknowledge ourselves as the spiritual beings we are. Granted, this is a bold and courageous step, but it is one that has been taken by all the women featured in this book, and millions more throughout time, from culture to culture. We do not step into our truest selves alone; we are in grand company.

Great gifts come to us when we acknowledge the Divine One within and live from the light of our truest selves. When we are able to acknowledge the foundation upon which the twelve Transformational Truths are based—My True Identity Is Spirit—the doorway to heaven on earth will open for us. When we can begin to embrace ourselves as women of Spirit, we are well on our way to living as the radiant creatures we were conceived to be eons ago in the heart and mind of God.

Reflection Questions

1. At this point in your journey, do you truly conceive of yourself as a spiritual being?
2. What disempowering messages do you experience through your ego self? What effects have those messages had upon your life? What steps have you taken to disengage from their influence?
3. How would you assess your ability to question any beliefs that have been handed to you?

Peaceful Pause

Embracing Yourself as Spirit

Close your eyes and relax. Feel your chest rising and falling. Listen to your breath moving in and out. Know that the breath that moves through you is divine, God's presence inside of you—giving you life—centering you in calm.

Remain focused on your breathing and notice the peaceful place it takes you to deep within. This is your real home. The calm that you feel is evidence that you have accessed your truest self in God. You *are* peace, you *are* love, you *are* happiness when you are in this place. As you settle more deeply into the sensations of your breath, feel the Divine One itself coming to rest in you. Trust this feeling of sacred presence within you. Know that you *are* spirit, a beautiful and unique manifestation of the greater Spirit, of God.

truth
one

I Am Free to Live a Spiritual Life of My Own Making

Joyce Rupp

The female soul is no small thing. Neither is a woman's right to define the sacred from a woman's perspective.

Sue Monk Kidd

God and I were not on speaking terms. I wasn't talking to *him*, listening to anything *he* had to say. "Don't talk to me about the 'G' word," I'd say to my friends, relegating God to outcast status. *He* had disappeared off my radar screen sometime in the mid-eighties, becoming nothing more than a blip that showed up in other people's conversations and lives. Not mine.

Finding Joyce Rupp changed all that. Through her writing, she gave me something I couldn't give myself: permission to explore a new relationship with the Divine that supported my emerging feminism. Despite growing up in the sixties, I hadn't been particularly interested in women's liberation. My only desire at that time was to live my own life, which meant, to me, marriage and a nice part-time career so I could have a family. Much to my surprise, after giving birth to three children, two of whom were girls, feminism crept in the back door of my rose-covered cottage. As a mother, I awoke one day to realize that despite the women's movement, the world was still inequitable and male dominated. I seemed to somehow lump God into the injustice of this, because

17

he is male (or so I'd been raised to believe) and could perhaps be a quiet complicitor in this charade of equality we'd been handed. A behind-the-times God wasn't fitting into my expanding feminist worldview.

Though I may have outwardly appeared irritated with God, beneath the surface ran a river of intense longing—a deep pool of desire to be in a meaningful relationship with the Divine. In the mid-1990s, after nearly seven years of feeling pretty much God-less, I found myself drawn to women's spirituality groups. I began to attend workshops and read books on the subject. As I did, I noticed that my spiritual frustration eased. I felt comfortable, at home, with a community of women, so much so that my friend Ellie and I decided on a whim to lease two rooms in an old Victorian house and create a women's spiritual growth center. We christened it The Gathering Place. Women came from miles around to explore their spiritual lives together. It was a glorious and enlivening time of connecting with women like ourselves who were searching for a spirituality that affirmed our feminine nature.

It was in the lending library of The Gathering Place that Joyce Rupp came into my life. Someone had donated one of her books, *A Star in My Heart*, to our cause. As I held her book in my hands, I sensed something wonderful was about to happen. What I found within its pages stunned and excited me. I learned that she had searched for a woman-friendly spirituality and found it. Not only found it, but reconfigured it for herself. Joyce Rupp had reshaped her spiritual life with a feminine hand that shook me to the core. She had given the Divine as she had come to understand it a whole new name—Sophia— Wisdom. As I read her words upon the page, I remember thinking, Oh, my. This is big. Really big. *Can you do that? Can you rename God for yourself? Is that even allowed?*

Reading those words, reading that name—Sophia—unleashed a maelstrom of feelings. Joy and terror, celebration and fear simultaneously swirled through me in a wild torrent. Joyce had arrived at the place I was trying so hard to get to myself. She had unearthed a connection with the Divine that enabled her to blossom as a woman, grow in faith, and embody the spiritual values she wished to express in the world. *I wanted that.* But could I possibly do the same as she did? I wondered. Did I have the strength? The courage? I didn't know, but I knew I had to give it a try. After all, with Joyce Rupp as my guide, how could I fail?

In that defining moment, a pilgrimage began, a barefooted trek into my soul to uncover a God of my own understanding. It was both thrilling and intimidating to embark in this way, for I had no idea how to start or which way to go. I learned later while reading *Dear Heart, Come Home* that Joyce had felt the same. She candidly confessed to bouts of self-doubt and great trepidation about her inner pilgrimages. "No map," she wrote in one of her journals. "No specific directions . . . how will I know where to go? How will I find my way? No map? But then my midlife soul whispers: 'There was a time before maps when pilgrims traveled by the stars.'"[1] I loved reading this passage. It was comforting to know that another woman had gone before me into uncharted territory guided only by her soul.

Every woman who has successfully embodied her holy woman self, in fact, has made such a pilgrimage. "As pilgrims," explains author Phil Cousineau, "we go back to find something we lost; we return to the source

to be restored, rejuvenated, revivified."[2] My personal
pilgrimage was destined to be one of casting off the religious attire I'd been handed as a young girl, remaking
it into a garment that fit my emerging self. As feminist
scholar Carol Lee Flinders describes it, "To become what
we would be, we must let go of everything we have
been."[3]

For many of us, this is what pilgrimage looks like. It
is an extensive time of sifting and sorting. We may be
familiar with religious beliefs or practices through our
family or community, but we may have outgrown them.
Or, perhaps, we never fully embraced them as our own.
Our personal pilgrimage becomes one of searching for
what *truly* nourishes us, what serves us and who we are
becoming. Of holding onto what feels right and letting
go of the rest. No matter what form our pilgrimage takes,
most of us come to this place of reckoning where we've
become increasingly uncomfortable with our spiritual
lives. A pilgrimage is launched to create a genuine spiritual expression of ourselves—one that resonates with us
on all levels—body, mind, heart, and soul.

The holy woman within us, somehow, mysteriously
hears this call to pilgrimage—knows it is time to "come
home." Joan Chittister maintains that it is God, the Spirit
within us, that is calling us to the deep conscious living
of a spiritual life.[4] The Spirit is alive and well within us,
calling us, even if we are not sure what that call will
mean or how to proceed. The desire we feel, that longing
to have a spiritual life that is truly representative of our
truest self, is the Holy One speaking through us, inviting
us into deeper relationship.

When we accept this invitation, our spiritual pilgrimage begins. This is the stepping-off place, the place that

for many of us feels the most uncertain on our inward trek because we are giving up the familiar to venture into the unknown. Though it may feel perilous at times, especially at the outset, thankfully there are experienced pilgrims to show us the way. Joyce Rupp is one such guide. She knows, perhaps better than any woman I have ever met, how to follow her inner compass on just such a trek. She is considered by many to be a "spiritual midwife"—one who helps us give birth to new versions of ourselves. She is gifted at midwifery because she has "rebirthed" her own true self so many times. She does so by going on inner pilgrimages, traveling deep into her heart and soul.

When the time came to write this chapter, I knew Joyce was the ideal guide for this topic, and I was thrilled when she agreed to speak with me. Though she describes herself as an introvert, I find her to be as warmhearted as she appears in her books and easy to talk to. Her presence is calming and steady, self-assured. I compliment her on her book, *Dear Heart, Come Home*, telling her how important it has been to me for my own mid-life journey. Her response surprises me. "I had so many fears about writing that book," she admits, "wondering if people thought I might be crazy. I jokingly said to a friend when it first came out that I felt like I wanted to put a paper bag over my head!"

I silently recall that she revealed similar hesitancy in an earlier correspondence we had about *Walk in a Relaxed Manner: Life Lessons from the Camino*—her book on personal pilgrimage. This pilgrimage, taken at age sixty, was of a physical nature. With her friend Tom, a retired priest, Joyce hiked five hundred miles through the Spanish Pyrenees along the famous pilgrimage route known as the Camino. It was arduous and simply life-changing. "I felt very vulnerable putting that one out there," she had said to me in that previous conversation.

Even in this early stage of our conversation, I am struck again by why I have repeatedly returned to Joyce's books for guidance. She gives me courage. She is honest and open, not afraid to admit her insecurities, and it is evident by her "spiritual success" that she has not been held back by them. She risks, ventures into the unknown, because she trusts the Divine enough to know she will be guided, protected, and victorious, no matter where the journey takes her. I'm especially eager to learn more about this bold journey of hers into a woman-friendly spirituality. I ask her to tell me more.

"It began in my mid-forties. There was a huge hole in my spiritual life," she reveals, "and I was looking for a suitable image for God. Discovering the feminine aspect of divinity was a major turning point for me." It happened for her when she read Riane Eisler's *The Chalice and the Blade*. "For the first time, the feminine movement made sense to me. I then read everything I could about goddesses and feminism. This led me, of course, to begin to see the huge chasm between the masculine and the feminine that existed in the Catholic Church. I found it increasingly difficult to tolerate exclusive language, for one, and male dominance by some priests and members of the hierarchy."

The feminine aspect of divinity of which Joyce speaks is an understanding that the Holy One inherently exhibits qualities that we attribute to the feminine. When the Divine is seen as possessing these qualities, we find that we may relate more easily because this image reflects what we are as women. Feminine qualities such as compassion are conveyed—openheartedness, receptivity, intuition, cooperation, inclusivity, and more.

An image of the sacred that affirms the feminine in this way is often referred to as "the feminine face of God." It is not a face those of us raised in traditional religions have witnessed very often, especially those of the West (Judaism, Christianity, and Islam). Joyce had not been raised with it. Neither had I. Instead, we were introduced to a God who was male; one who possessed very dominant personality traits. God often seemed judgmental, powerful, controlling, exclusive, even disappointed or angry with us as human beings. This was also an image of God who was perceived as outside of and distant from ourselves.

Joyce shares with me how she finally came to connect with the feminine face of God. She describes her ongoing fascination with the wisdom presented in biblical scripture. She found herself naturally drawn to explore it more deeply, enough to want to write a book on the subject. By her own admission, she had no intimate knowledge of the biblical Wisdom books themselves. One day, when reading a passage in Proverbs that described a beautiful figure playing before God, something struck a chord, drawing her closer. Thus began an ardent search into who this celebratory partner of the Holy One named Sophia—the Greek word for "Wisdom"—might be.

"There she was," explains Joyce, "sitting in the Jewish scriptures all my life and I had never noticed her. When I embraced Sophia, I felt I had finally come home to my truest self. She filled in the huge hole in my spiritual life that had been there because of the lack of a feminine image for the Divine. Sophia became guide and companion to me."

In our searching for a spirituality that fits our emerging sacred self, we should not be surprised if the feminine face of God makes an appearance, just as it did for Joyce. We'll recognize "her" by an unmistakable tug on our heartstrings. A subtle knowing felt deep within the recesses of our being that we are, for no particular reason, welcome here. We may experience this as a sense of "breathing room," warmth, or comfort.

I am fascinated to learn how it was Joyce knew that Sophia was the right connection for her. Why Sophia and not another representation of the Divine? After all, there are so many one could choose from or connect with. She clarifies, "I began by reading and meditating each day on one of the scripture passages referring to Holy Wisdom." As she prayerfully dwelt inside the wisdom literature, she came to a personal relationship with Sophia. "I moved from viewing 'wisdom' as a quality of the Divine One to perceiving 'Wisdom' as the Divine One herself. It was then that I began naming Sophia as the One for whom I had longed."

What I am hearing Joyce say is that she found an image of God in Sophia that allowed her to embrace her own femininity—and one in which the Divine embraced her feminine nature in return. Marion Woodman, a Jungian analyst whose writings I've enjoyed over the years, might describe it this way: "The eternal Feminine is that loving, cherishing, nurturing principle which looks at the life that is becoming and honors it, celebrates it, allows it to grow into its full maturity. . . . The task of the feminine is to contain, as the mother contains the baby."[5]

No wonder Joyce, along with the rest of us, may feel subtly drawn to a divine connection that is feminine—one that contains, holds, and nurtures us. We ourselves are "born nurturers": We are physically, psychologically, emotionally, and culturally programmed to nurture and care for others. Because of this, a feminine image of the Divine would feel "natural"—a reflection of our innermost selves.

It was out of this new awareness that Joyce wrote her first book on Sophia, *A Star in My Heart*. She tells me that this felt like an enormous risk to her, a sort of "coming out," because she was not sure she would be accepted by her Catholic readers. "What I found has astounded me," she says. "Many have said something similar to what I experienced. Finding Sophia is like a 'coming home,' 'a finding of a long awaited friend,' 'a deep connection with sacred wonder and with mystery.'"

Sophia has become the best divine name for Joyce's prayers, but it may not necessarily be our own. It is the name that she prays with that takes her deeper into her truest self. Sophia represents the presence that offers guidance, truth, and companionship to and through Joyce. For Sophia is not an anthropomorphic figure in the sky, an "other" who lives outside of her, but an indwelling aspect of God who just happens to have a feminine persona. Joyce believes it is very important for us to give an actual name to the Divine One with whom we enter into relationship, because without a name, our connection may remain distant and impersonal.

And how will we know that name? Mahatma Gandhi explained it for us this way: "If we have listening ears, God speaks to us in our own language, whatever that language is." Said another way, we must learn to pay attention and listen very, very carefully, just as Joyce has.

Creating an authentic spiritual life for ourselves requires true contemplation—*a deep and profound ability to listen to the Spirit as it speaks to and through us.* The root meaning of the word contemplation means to "make a temple with." I take this to mean that it is our soul-bound duty to create a temple within ourselves to clearly perceive the Divine as it is making itself known to us. A temple is a place dedicated to the worship or presence of a deity. Our body—its mind and heart—can serve as that temple. It is our own inner sanctuary and, by necessity, a place of profound stillness. A place where the holy can be experienced, recognized, and, ultimately, embraced. It is up to each one of us to create this temple within.

We begin by making sacred space within ourselves, through silence, so we can be more open and receptive to the Divine as it shows up. A personal practice of stillness enables us to listen, *truly* listen, so we can hear how the Sacred One is revealing itself. We lean into God with attuned senses so we can notice what is being communicated. Divine communication takes many forms—words, sounds, sights, sensations. It takes practice to notice these expressions and to listen for their import. It takes discernment.

Discernment is a learned process of sifting and sorting characterized by deep listening and feeling. It is the method we use to determine whether something that comes into our experience is meant to be incorporated into our spiritual life or not. It is not necessarily a rational process, but one that is sourced in the heart's wisdom—in knowing. Joyce tells me that her earliest discernment of God's presence began when she was a child living on a farm in rural northwest Iowa.

"It was a wonderful experience for me to be able to spend time in the woods, roam the fields, play under the stars. I easily sensed the divine presence with me. The presence was comforting, caring," she says. "Nature was my companion and friend. Through nature, the Divine was in my heart and in the world."

However, Joyce did not speak about her God connection through nature for many years. "There was always the strong warning from the Church that pagans worshipped nature and that this was sinful." But it was in nature that Joyce spoke with God and felt an assuring guidance. "The stars pulled me toward something deep and strong, toward a sense that I was protected, loved, and guided."

As happens with many of us, we lack trust in our heart wisdom. We listen to the "superior," rational wisdom of others and doubt our inner knowing. Joyce admits that this happened to her. As a result, over the years she fell away from her sacred connection to nature. "When I finally gained my courage to speak out on behalf of Sophia, I regained my sense of the sacred in nature that had been lost in childhood. Today, I no longer worry about what theology might say about nature and the Divine. I just enjoy the sacred presence I find there."

It takes time, patience, and faithfulness to shape an authentic spirituality for ourselves. Joyce admits hers has taken a lifetime to sculpt. I believe Joyce would concur with Gandhi, who offered an important piece of advice for us in these early stages of discernment: "As long as you derive inner help and comfort from anything, keep it." And what does not, I'm sure he would add, leave behind. This is how we initially know to explore something further or not. We begin to notice and feel its effect upon us. We learn to listen, to hold our experience, and to watch how, through time, it takes us into a greater daily experience of Spirit and our own wholeness, or takes us further away.

It is evident throughout my conversation with Joyce that she has become a master of discernment. She explains to me how in her twenties she chose to enter the Servants of Mary community to become a nun. She was determined, even at that early age, not to stay in the community if it didn't resonate with her. Forty years later, she's still there, primarily she says, because of her own community of women who have supported her perpetual seeking and spiritual growth. In later years, her discernment included a two-year course of study at Naropa University, a Buddhist university in Boulder, Colorado, and further study elsewhere to earn a master's degree in transpersonal psychology. "My faith stretched and grew stronger wings because of these experiences."

If we are to reclaim ourselves as holy women, each of must engage a spirituality of our own making. "Don't be satisfied with poems and stories of how things have gone with others," advises the Persian poet Rumi. "Unfold your own myth." A myth, in this sense, is nothing more than the story of who God is to us, who we are to God, and how we personally experience that unique connection. It is up to us to fashion our own, just as Joyce has.

We can engage in this process by exploring what image of the Divine feels most desirable to us, just as Joyce has. It will likely be an image to which we are naturally drawn because it provides comfort and healing. This is where deep listening and discernment comes in. We ask ourselves, "What is it within us that this image of God will transform from wounded to whole?" For example, if we hunger for a mother or father, we may perceive God as a caring Parent who is ever-present, a provider, or a nurturer. If we perceive ourselves in need of forgiveness, we may image God as Forgiver, a God of mercy and compassion. If we are in need of a faithful companion, God is Friend to us, and we are lonely no more. Because Joyce and I had each struggled with a masculine image of God, we opened ourselves to experiencing God in a new way—one less masculine and more feminine. One that was nurturing, unconditionally loving, and capable of intimacy.

With Joyce as "the wind beneath my wings," I was finally able to accept the invitation to unfold my own myth and name God for myself. Over the years, I had been deeply drawn to an image of God as Mother, the Great Comforter, the Mother of Us All. The presence of God who provided solace felt, to me, like the Blessed Mother Mary herself. Over a ten-year period, I journeyed deeper into the heart of Mother Mary. I was not Catholic and knew very little about her or what she has meant to countless others. In time, she has become my guide and companion, my comforter and protector. She is the name for the Divine that brings me into deeper communion with an indwelling God.

The particular image of God that we hold will become the great determiner of how we live in the world and relate to others. If God is a loving Parent, we will likely nurture those around us. If God is Forgiver, we will show kindness toward others. If God is Friend, we will be a faithful companion to those in need. The opposite is true as well. Harsh, cold, or punishing images of the Divine foster a judgmental, fear-based spirituality that we will make manifest in the world.

This is what is meant by embodied spirituality. This is what a holy woman ultimately seeks on her pilgrimage. She desires connection with a God who lives and breathes through her so lovingly, so supportively, that she, in turn, will be able to express those same qualities to others.

The unique spirituality that we create for ourselves— whether it be an image of God as Father, God as Mother, God as Nature—is of no importance, really, if we believe that our connection to him/her/it is a true and valid expression for us. Joyce reminds us, "All our names for the Divine, whether male or female, are inadequate. All these metaphors are our feeble human attempts and projections as we try to draw near to the Mysterious One."[6]

"Whenever I am with women today," she adds, "I ask them to trust their inner wisdom and to believe that their own journey is a valid and beautiful journey."[7] By her unfailing dedication to her search for an authentic divine connection, Joyce Rupp personifies for us the first Transformational Truth:

I Am Free to Live a Spiritual Life of My Own Making

Creating a deeply personal spirituality for herself is at the root of all Joyce does, and this is what I admire about her the most. "Turning again and again to what gives me life and vitality," she says, is the key. She has remained faithful to her journey, no matter where it has taken her or how risky it has been. As a result, the spiritual lessons and rewards have been plentiful.

In honor of her sixtieth birthday, Joyce chose to embark on perhaps her greatest, most challenging pilgrimage yet—walking the Camino de Santiago. It was a grueling journey for her, carrying everything she needed for the thirty-seven-day trek in a twenty-pound pack on her back. With aching backs and feet, she and her friend Tom hiked up and down mountain passes, through rain and cold, not knowing for certain where they would sleep or from where their next meal might come. As I read *Walk in a Relaxed Manner*, I marveled at her resilience, her faithfulness. I was deeply touched by her candid admissions to feeling depression, anger, or judgment of others she met along the way. Each tussle with her false self turned into a chapter in the book—a powerful lesson for positive living. One chapter in particular touched my heart more deeply than the rest. It was how Joyce chose, at one point, to walk the route—a metaphor for her life—in an entirely new way.

Early on in their pilgrimage, she and Tom noticed their tendency to push themselves, to pressure themselves to get to the next *refugio* (a sleeping place set aside for pilgrims) to ensure they had a bed for the night; to keep pace with other pilgrims who were younger, in better shape than they were. They often set high goals for themselves of walking many more miles a day than may have been wise. This caused physical suffering, stress, and detached awareness of what was going on around them, as well as within. In a moment of clarity, they realized they were not being present to their own pilgrimage.

Joyce recalled the wise advice of a friend who had walked the Camino a few years before. He had reminded her to drink plenty of water and *to walk in a relaxed manner*. From that moment on, they slowed down, tended to themselves—body, mind, and spirit—and savored this precious, once-in-a-lifetime experience. "We discovered that our outer action of slowing down our walking also influenced our inner tempo. We grew more peaceful," she wrote, "and enjoyed our time with other pilgrims instead of envying their fast walking strides. The beauty of the Spanish countryside took on deeper color and hue. Its people seemed to grow friendlier by the day. We worried less and were more at home with ourselves and one another."[8]

What a powerful testimony for our own pilgrimage— this journey into our sacred selves. How simple it sounds! Slow down. Enjoy. Notice the magic, the mystery of life. *Walk in a relaxed manner.* For when we do, profound growth can be ours. "The journey itself," Joyce reminds us, "is of prime importance. . . . It is how we live, how we respond to what life brings us, that creates the difference in our spiritual journey. . . . The process of being spiritually transformed into our truest selves happens all along the way."[9]

Knowing this, let us bestow a pilgrim's blessing upon ourselves. May we travel well. May we enjoy the journey. May the star in our own heart guide us home, as it has Joyce, to the God of our understanding.

Reflection Questions

1. Where are you on the journey of a spirituality of your own making? Have you given yourself wholehearted permission to do so?
2. Have you consciously named the Divine One, especially in light of your emerging self?
3. If you have been able to name the Divine One, what qualities does he/she/it have? What qualities does it invite you to cultivate in yourself for greater expression in the world?

Peaceful Pause

Welcoming the Divine One In

Close your eyes and take one deep, cleansing breath. Then bring your attention to your in-breath and your out-breath. Allow each one to slow down, soften, and ease you into feelings of relaxation.

When you feel sufficiently at ease, with each in-breath, silently say:

> I welcome you in, Divine One. I welcome
> you into my mind, my body, my heart, my
> life.

Repeat as many times as you like. As you do so, imagine a space opening up inside of you where the Divine One can dwell. A resting place where God can make him/her/itself known to you. A sanctuary. A temple within in the region of your heart. Experience your in-breath and your out-breath moving slowly, like a sweet vapor drifting through this sacred space. Blessing it. Sanctifying it. Making it holy ground for the Divine One to be housed within you.

Finally, give thanks for this sacred place that exists within you. A place you have specially prepared with your breath and set aside for the Holy One to make itself known to you. Enjoy the temple of your own being and dwell there as long as you desire, anytime you desire.

truth
two

I Trust My Body's Divine Connection

Jan Phillips

If anything is sacred, the human body is.
Walt Whitman

Like a moth to a flame, I was drawn to visit mission after mission in Southern California. San Juan Capistrano, Santa Barbara, San Diego, and La Purisima. Sometimes I felt like Alice in Wonderland, a stranger in a strange land, overwhelmed by sights and sounds both mesmerizing and confusing, yet pulled magnetically forward into the mystery of these places by an unnamed "something."

The blessed silence of each place worked its magic upon me, and I was swept into a realm of pure feeling. All thinking stopped; my senses were vibrantly alive. It felt so *good* to be there. So right. My body firm and safe against a hard, wooden pew. The quiet atmosphere, imbued with peace, stilled all thoughts, soothed every ligament and muscle with a balm of calm.

And then it would begin. A warm, syrupy shower of love, starting from the crown of my head, running down my skin, coursing through my veins. A divine wash. I'd bask in the feelings of love and comfort that were created, and tears would begin to flow—rivulets of relief. For I knew, deep within the recesses of my being, that I was home in God. And God was at home in me.

~~~

    To be able to experience the Divine One moving in and through me in everyday life, as it did when I visited the missions, has been a journey of many years. I remember feeling it as a young girl while sitting in church, walking through my grandmother's garden, or lying beneath the stars at camp. It was a deep knowing that "surely God is in this place," as the song goes. That Spirit was all around me, radiating through stained-glass windows, flowers, or constellations and, at the same time, within me, experienced through my body, if I would allow myself to feel it.

    As a woman on pilgrimage to her truest self, I can't help but wonder what happened along the way. Where did I lose, where do any of us lose, that divine connection we may have felt through our bodies as young women? I believe it happens in early adolescence when we became overtly conscious of our physical selves.

    In our preteen years, we begin to doubt, even distrust, our bodies. Bellies and breasts are changing, not to mention that great mysterious divide, the juncture between our thighs, hidden, dark with mystery. We are being transformed into someone else without our conscious involvement or permission. Is it a wonder that at this formative period of our lives we begin to develop suspicion about our bodies?

    Combine this self-doubt with societal and religious implications that our bodies are bad (a source of temptation), inferior (the "weaker sex"), and flawed (in need of improvement), and we have a good case for amnesia, forgetting our body as a conduit to the Divine. For centuries now, we've internalized these messages, so it is not surprising that most women truly dislike and mistrust their bodies.

It has been reported that 75 percent of American women are dissatisfied with their appearance. Fifty percent are on a diet at any given time.[1] I know this to be true firsthand, because I was one of those women. Like so many others, I've fallen prey to the myth perpetuated to the female gender that we are somehow physically inferior, in need of beautifying and perfecting.

From adolescence on, it seems, our bodies are not our friends: They are enemies we wage war against through diets, radical exercise programs, cosmetic enhancement, even surgery. We may believe that our bodies betray us again and again. They do not look or behave like we think they should: They gain weight; miscarry or are infertile; cyclically rage (PMS/menopause); sag, fall out, fall apart through aging; become chronically sick or ravaged with disease—all without our having a say in the matter. Who can trust a "friend" who acts like that?

Knowing this, what a stretch of the imagination it is for us to conceive of our bodies as sacred! To believe they are magnificent containers created by the Divine to house our souls on earth. And, perhaps, even more important than this, that our bodies are a direct means of communication with our Source.

Yet it is only through our bodies that we can have a truly intimate relationship with God. Our mind, which can conceive of God through thought, is housed within our brain. Our senses—sight, hearing, and smell—provide the stuff of which our thoughts and feelings about the world are made. Our sense of touch, along with internal body responses—heartbeat and breath—attune us to the world outside of our bodies, alerting us there is something of significance there. Our lips give voice to this experience. Our hands and feet creatively express our understanding of this experience. Our bodies, therefore, are the ultimate vehicle through which we communicate with the Divine. This vessel, this body, is a sacred conduit for the flow of Spirit.

The journey into our truest selves is dependent upon our ability to realize that our bodies are sacred. As Jay Michaelson, author of *God in Your Body*, writes, "Realization is simply waking up. And the body, because it is always present here and now, is both the best vehicle for doing so . . . and how holiness expresses itself in the world."[2] Michaelson goes on to say that our greatest spiritual achievement on a personal level is not to transcend the body (as some spiritual systems would advocate), but to fully embrace it, to join the body and spirit together so we are, at last, whole human beings, not fragmented versions of ourselves.

Living as our truest selves requires that we wake up to our bodies as the magnificent creations they are. We *can* learn to love and trust them again, enough to be our guides back to a healthy and holy perception of self. For it is in the body, says author Jan Phillips, that heaven and earth meet. "The journey of our lives is a journey of remembering and reconnecting. . . . We feel the Beloved in every cell, sense the sacred one in every heartbeat, every touch, every image our eyes encounter, every sound our ears behold."[3]

So how do we begin what may feel like a potentially tumultuous journey back into our bodies to reclaim them as sacred? We take the hand of a woman who has done so herself and allow her to show us how. Jan Phillips is a teacher, an award-winning photographer, and an author, who, as you will soon learn, has successfully recreated a loving relationship with her body after a lifetime of woundedness. She has done so primarily through a process she calls Divining the Body, and she has, thankfully, recorded her process in a book from which we can all benefit.

Jan Phillips came into my life at a precipitous point, when I was beginning to express myself through writing. She was a consummate writer, so I spent time with her through her books, for they seemed to model who I could ultimately be. Jan was a unique blend of intellect and soul; a contemplative monastic, yet worldly activist; a truly compassionate human being who seemed to embody the wholeness (and holiness) I was seeking. Plus, she was a darn good writer! And I certainly wanted to be that.

In 1997 I was deep into the process of writing my first book, and my nasty inner critic was quite vocal, constantly berating me, telling me I had no business trying to write a book at all. In a particularly bleak moment, I called my editor, Nessa, desperate for advice on how to continue writing when everything inside me said to stop. "Have you read *Marry Your Muse* by Jan Phillips?" she asked. "'The Artist's Creed' should take care of everything."

Nessa was right. Reading Jan's inspiring words to the struggling artist within reduced me to grateful tears and cured my creative woes. In moments, I was back on track again. Her words, "I believe I am worth the time it takes to create whatever I feel called to create," became a mantra for me.[4] In that moment, I adopted Jan (though she didn't know it) as the guardian angel of my own muse.

So when an invitation came to interview her in 2004, I jumped at the chance. I conducted a phone interview with her first; then we met in person a few months later. We shared a delightful afternoon together at the Inn at the Rustic Gate in Big Rapids, Michigan, where Jan was offering her weekend seminar on Divining the Body.

We meet on a scorching day, one of the hottest of the summer, and Jan, barefooted, looking like a kid ready to head outside and play, greets me in the entryway of the inn. Her dark hair is a riot of curls from the heat, and I like her ordinariness immediately. She holds no pretenses. She has a body presence that says, "I'm comfortable with who I am."

To see this quality of "alrightness with self" in a woman is a rarity. She has none of the self-consciousness most of us have about our bodies, so consumed with how we look. By the way Jan holds herself, with confidence of bearing, she conveys the energy of wholeness I'd sensed over the telephone a few months earlier. I had wondered how she'd arrived at this place of comfort with her body. I hope to find out now.

Fortified with tall glasses of iced tea to combat the heat, we head to the library of the inn, a small, comfortable room lined with bookshelves and soft chairs, ideal for an intimate conversation. We settle in and quickly come to the heart of the matter: How can women today divine the body to reconnect with their sacred selves? It is Jan's sharing of her childhood experience of spirituality that offers me a rare glimpse into a young girl's loss and recovery of the sacred through her body.

"When I learned prior to my First Communion that my body was a temple for the Holy Ghost," she begins, "I thought, 'It is? Really? Wow! This is good news!' Right near your heart, I was told, is this little flame, and that flame is the God flame. I was really thrilled that inside of my own body was a chunk of God. Part of a star that had broken off. It was fiery and alive. So for me, as a child, it wasn't a belief of not having a divine potential because I knew I had the flame within me."

But as Jan's story reveals, it was a childhood of confusing messages that began to shadow this spark in her. She tells me that she knew her body was here in service of her soul, but "the problem was it was the very same church that informed me I was a temple of God that also informed me that by being a woman I was the source of all sin. This body of yours, I was told, is a container of dangerous elements. You are suspect, a perpetrator, and your body is a source of sin. Don't have a good time with your body, don't enjoy it, don't touch it. Don't get intimate with it, and don't let anyone else get intimate with it, either.

"That was such a terrible mixed message to tell a child, and it confused the hell out of me because I was truly seeking to become the best little Christ I could be. Even before my teen years, I was on the path to finding my own divinity and reading *The Imitation of Christ* by Thomas à Kempis every day. I believed what I was told by 'the holy people.' I became more and more torn asunder because I equated holiness with everything that was not the body."

This mixed theology of a woman's body as both sacred and profane contributed to the confusion Jan was beginning to feel in her own body. She relates to me that growing up she didn't feel like other girls. She didn't want to stay inside and play with dolls, as was expected of her; she wanted to be a boy and do "boy things."

Despite her inner turmoil, Jan stayed faithful to her desire to embrace her divinity by entering the convent at age eighteen. She describes the two years she spent there as "an all-heaven-breaking-loose experience," offering a lifestyle that cracks her heart open with joy, "because there were no men or power struggles, and I felt safe, so I could rise like cream in a community of women." Days were characterized by solitude, community, prayer, and service, the things she loved, still loves, and to this day bases her life upon. Yet there was pain in the convent, as well.

It was 1966, she says, and there was no gay consciousness. "All I knew was that I was very different. The Church said terrible things about homosexuals. I would look in different dictionaries to find the word 'homosexual' or 'lesbian,' wondering if anyone might say anything good about it because I thought I might be one. I thought, 'But I'm trying really hard to be like Christ. I am full of God, and I just *can't* be evil.' I knew that." This confusion tore Jan apart and caused terrible sorrow, but she had no way to transform that sorrow into awareness.

"Imagine a young woman going to live with a community of only women, and there is no conversation about what you do with your emotions." As she speaks, her eyes fill with tears. "What do you do with your passions? What do you do with your body, in lieu of what everyone else is doing with their bodies? I am in a holy and sacred place, but there is no conversation about this," she says. "Not even sublimation. Nothing about our bodies. I had no idea of what to do." With that painful admission, Jan begins to cry, covering her face with her hands.

I am not prepared for how raw her feelings are, how much hurt she still carries because of these early experiences. I find myself offering a silent prayer for her comfort. I am not completely surprised by her response, though, because I know when any of us has been misled or misunderstood—emotionally or physically—especially when we are very young, the pain is housed within our bodies for years. It is through testifying to it—giving voice, sound, and timbre to the hurt—that we release it from the body so we can heal. But such healing does not happen overnight, and sometimes not even in thirty years, as Jan attests by her sharing.

She takes a deep breath, wiping her eyes, and continues to tell me she was asked to leave the convent. It is an unexpected and devastating blow to her, one for which reasons were never offered except to say that she did not have "a religious disposition."

As our conversation continues, I am relieved to learn that twenty-two years later, Jan garnered the courage to return to the order to gain closure about this disabling event. She was offered an apology for the years of pain that had been caused by this misjudgment, and she finally began to heal.

It has been an emotional recounting for Jan, so we decide to pause and take a break. When we begin again, I'm eager to know how she healed the rift between her body and the sacred. How can any of us do the same?

As she explains it, we begin by "crawling back into our body." We approach our body in a new way, no matter what our history is with it. This means acknowledging that our body is where our wisdom lives, where a sacred experience of life can be felt. "In our hearts, in our hands and legs; wisdom comes from the places I have walked to," Jan says, "from the places I have cried, from the people I have touched, from the stories I have listened to, from the things my eyes have seen. Through my senses, the holy has entered into my being. Through my senses, the holy is expressed into the world."

Crawling back into our body can begin anywhere, as Jan demonstrates in *Divining the Body*, and is a different process for everyone. One way is to spend time with the various parts of our body with which we have difficulty or low regard. Each chapter of her book is brilliantly dedicated to a specific body part that can be sacramentalized—healed and loved back into sacred connection. We can begin by attending to our wounded areas first, whether it be feet, hands, the back, our sexual organs, the breasts, the heart, the voice, the eyes, or the ears. We begin by slowing down, paying attention to that body part, and recreating a positive relationship with it.

With Jan's wise book guiding me, I'd explored this process with my own body—addressing one particular body part I'd come to dislike—my belly. I'd given birth to three children (and miscarried two), and my midsection was uncooperative about returning to its taut, pre-pregnant condition, no matter how much I dieted or exercised. Jan's wise and comforting words helped me make peace with my abdomen. I rubbed it tenderly with strokes of affection and talked to it lovingly through positive affirmations, as she suggested. My relationship with my belly shifted when I began to view it—its softness and bulge—as evidence of its ability to have conceived and given birth to three beautiful children. A lasting peace was forged as I became grateful for my belly and thanked it for all the years of good service it had given me.

We must each find our own pathway back into the body. The way can be gentle if we listen to the body's urgings and tend to its needs. But most of us do not listen because we are not highly attuned to the body's communication. And even if we were more attuned, it is not likely we would heed its call, for we have not yet experienced our body as a friend— or as trustworthy. However, if we refuse to listen, an involuntary path of reentry may be thrust upon us. We are forcibly awakened, mightily shaken into awareness that something in our body, our world, our sacred connection is amiss.

Sue Monk Kidd writes in *The Dance of the Dissident Daughter*, "Here is one of the principles of women waking: If you don't respond to the first gentle nudges, they will increase with intensity. Next you will wake up on the roof. And if you do not respond to that, there will likely be a crash."[5] My conversation with Jan reveals that this is precisely what happened to her. A crash of a dramatic nature, one that debilitated her. It forced her to crawl back into the body from which she had been so disconnected since childhood.

One day in 2002, while standing in front of her car on the side of the road videotaping a flock of birds, Jan's vehicle was hit by another car, and she was thrown into a field. Her car, with its burning muffler, landed on top of her. Just as she was mentally preparing for what felt like impending death, two men spotted her car. They saw her alive under the wreckage and offered to get help. "You are the help," she cried out. "Just lift up the car." Somehow, miraculously, they did.

Jan survived the accident, but received third-degree burns all over her back and hip that required painful skin graft surgery. After the surgery, she could barely move. She could do nothing but lie very, very still. In this enforced stillness, she started to notice things about her body. "It began with observing the most exquisite difference in my feelings about what I was going to put into my body because I could hardly move. I had to lay so still," she explains. "I've never been one who was highly conscious about what I put into my body. If I wanted a hot fudge sundae, then I'd eat it; if I wanted half a bottle of wine, I'd drink it. For the first time in my life I didn't experience very much hunger, but whenever I had need of food I found myself only wanting something really good." She would say to her partner, Annie, who helped in her recovery, "I just want a glass of water, one-half an apple, a couple slices of cheese. Just small amounts of things."

Jan began a process of listening intently to what her body was feeling, needing, for wholeness. "It was as if my *cells* were looking at the menu, not me and my mind. My cells were looking at the possibility of healing by saying to me, 'This is what I want to drink, to eat.' For weeks and weeks my body directed me, and I listened. It was a very holy experience for me to feel how my body took over leadership at that time."

Psychological healing from the accident came next. Jan began to feel anxiety; she was afraid to sleep because she would experience the danger of the accident all over again—being hit from behind by a car without any warning. Jan continued to listen to her body for guidance, for how to give it the assistance it needed to heal her emotional injuries. She went from healer to healer, engaging all sorts of body/mind therapies. Each therapy brought some level of change in body energy or perception, but respite from her body anxiety was not complete until she was led to a bioenergetic therapist.

What Jan learned from this therapist was to communicate with her body and its parts. She learned to talk to her back, because her back had not injured her, but saved her. She learned to talk to all of the other parts of her body, too, expressing gratitude for how they had served her over the years. And as she did, the anxiety-producing energy bound up within her cells and organs began to shift and move out. The anxiety she'd been plagued with disappeared, and healing was finally able to take place on all levels. Most importantly, she learned, "My body was here in service of my spirit."

Getting back in touch with her body through the medium of injury and pain enabled Jan to listen to its wise counsel. She gave her body what it asked for to be well: rest, quiet, moderation, healing touch, loving thoughts, gratitude. And her body responded in kind, opening her to a vibrant new experience of the body as sacred.

I believe that we do not have to "crash and burn" as Jan did to reconnect with our bodies. Instead, I believe that by careful, intuitive listening we can foster a sacred partnership with it. This listening can only begin, however, when we are able to slow down enough to pay attention, to create sacred space within ourselves and become quiet enough to hear what our bodies want and need to bring themselves—and us—into greater wholeness. For the Spirit will generally not scream at us (at least not until we've been given many subtle cues that have been ignored). Its method of communication is gentle: a whisper, a color, a touch, a tone, a flutter of the heart. "Come show yourself to my soul in ever-new ways," wrote the poet Rabindranath Tagore. "Come in scents, come in hues, come in songs. Let my body thrill with joy at Your Touch." If there is a cacophony of noise and confusion within us, we likely will not hear the Spirit's call or feel its touch.

In my own life, I would not have been able to have a "felt" experience of sacred presence (like I experienced at the missions and other sacred sites) if I had not cultivated practices that showed me how to make the connection. I had to relearn how to allow my body to be a conduit for the Divine. One such practice that can reintroduce us to the feeling capacity of our body/mind is to spend time with our breath. By venturing back into the body through the simple act of breathing, we can cultivate heightened awareness that the body is a receptacle for the indwelling Spirit.

Like Jan, at one point in my life, I began to experience anxiety. I consulted a naturopathic physician about a "cure." She prescribed two twenty-minute-a-day periods of rest and deep breathing. By accessing the quiet—doing nothing but listening to and feeling my breath move in and out of my body—inner peace and calm began to flow in, and the anxiety began to diminish.

During these rest periods, as I fully engaged with my breath—breathing in and out, slowly, gently—I had a sense that something very holy was happening. Through the simple movement of air through my nostrils, lungs, and limbs, I was being restored. There was sacredness in this breath—I could feel it. I knew that God was breathing in and through me. It was not until years later I learned that the word "breath" is linked to the notion of "spirit." The Hebrew word for spirit is *ruach*, and ruach can also mean "breath" or "wind." In other languages, as well, the word for spirit is also the word for breath. In Latin, *spiritus*. In Sanskrit, *pragna*. *Pneuma* in Greek.[6]

Heightening our physical senses is another way we can begin to connect with the Divine through the body, but it is one we will likely have to relearn. We live in a world that bombards us with stimuli; most of us experience sensory overload on a daily basis. There is too much noise, too many things that vie for our attention; so many and so much that our senses can actually shut down. We numb out, dumb out, and, over time, our senses become dim, unattuned to the environment around us. We become desensitized.

Getting back in touch with the glorious instruments of our senses can usher in a whole new experience of the Divine. We can experience the Sacred One who is present in all things if we have the eyes to see, ears to hear, hands to touch. We can learn to "pay attention on purpose," to resensitize ourselves by carefully noticing what is all around us. (We will explore this more deeply through mindfulness practices in "I Cultivate Compassion for Myself" with Sue Patton Thoele.)

It was through the art of photography that Jan was able to return to her body and its senses in yet another way. As a young girl, she loved looking through the family photographs her mother had placed in a shoebox. The photos soothed and calmed her. In her book on photography as healing art, *God Is at Eye Level*, she describes how looking through the lens of a camera helped her hone "the act of focusing, being totally attentive. When I look through my lens now, focused only on what is before me, I am grounded and healed. . . . My vision is clear, and I am one with whatever I am looking at, as I was one with those images forty years ago. . . . Full of joy, as we all can be, when we look with the eyes of a child, in rapt attention."[7]

"There is nothing to learn, but much to unlearn," Jan writes. "It is not facts we need more of, but feelings. We need to learn how to return to our senses, to reenter our bodies and allow what is within to flow through and out of us."[8] Through her own healing journey, Jan Phillips testifies to the power of the second Transformational Truth:

I Trust My Body's Divine Connection

To connect with our truest selves requires that we heal our relationship with our bodies. We vow to do whatever it takes to crawl back into our bodies so we can live there—gloriously—like goddesses in the temples of old. With self-directed passion, we can repair the wounds of body, mind, and heart, just as Jan has. We stop abusing our bodies by overeating, overworking, and stressing ourselves. We stop ascribing to impossible standards of perfection. We do whatever it takes to honor, trust, and love our bodies again. In time, the rift between our bodies and the Spirit will heal and the unconditional friendship we had with our bodies as young girls will return.

As we hug and say our goodbyes at the inn, I marvel at the woman with whom I've just shared a soulful afternoon. If Jan only knew what I'm seeing right now, I think to myself. For who I see standing here in front of me is not a middle-aged woman who has journeyed long and hard to embody her truest self, but a vibrant, curly-haired little girl, aglow with life and love and God.

In this very moment, Jan Phillips, to me, is a holy and whole expression of divinity on earth.

Today as I reminisce about our encounter, an important truth conveyed by the great yogi Paramahansa Yogananda comes to mind: "Matter was created, not to repress God, but to express God." Indeed, we are that, flesh and blood expressions of the Holy One who lives in and through each one of us. The one who sees through our eyes, hears through our ears, creates through our hands, moves through our feet. May we express well, through our body, the Sacred One within.

Reflection Questions

1. How would you describe your current relationship with your body? What feelings do you have about it on a day-to-day basis?
2. Is there a particular body part you would like to make peace with?
3. How have you experienced the Divine in your unique way through your senses? Through your mind? Through your heart?

Peaceful Pause

Blessing the Body

Lie down on your back in a comfortable, quiet place. Close your eyes and place your hand on your midsection and feel it rise and fall gently along with your breath. Inhale and exhale, slowly and evenly, relaxing your mind and body.

Identify a particular part of your body with which you would like to develop a loving relationship. It may be a part of you that, in this moment, feels tense or is in pain, or it may be one you have struggled with emotionally. Continuing to breathe in a relaxed manner, place your palm on that spot. Imagine that you are sending warmth, a soothing color, or healing energy into it. You may choose to tenderly rub that area with a delicate, circular motion. Communicate lovingly with it through your own gentle, accepting touch.

Now begin to send that portion of your body loving thoughts—thoughts of comfort, peace, and well-being. Offer it feelings of acceptance and gratitude. With each out-breath say, "I appreciate you. I thank you for serving me well over the years. I honor and bless you." In your own way, end by giving thanks for your body, this magnificent and loyal temple that houses your soul.

truth
three

I Choose Thoughts and Feelings That Honor My Sacred Self

Iyanla Vanzant

*May my mind every morning become as beautiful
as hope-dawn-rays.*

Sri Chinmoy

What can I say about a woman who makes a majesty of her life, a woman who has come from such woeful beginnings that your heart breaks in the hearing of it; who survived a painful childhood and a battered and bruised adulthood, yet rises like a phoenix from the ashes of her life to dwell among the stars? I can't help but wonder what special insights she might possess to be so resilient, so victorious.

If you had the opportunity to ask her that question yourself, as I did for the purpose of a magazine interview, you would be heartened by her response: "I believe the highest service you can give to God is taking care of yourself. Begin to learn to honor yourself, your mind, your talents, your gifts and abilities, and then use them to support yourself and others," she says. "It doesn't matter how you do it—as a barmaid, lawyer, housewife, or bus driver." With her signature contagious humor, she reveals the secret of her success: "I just keep flappin' my wings, and you can too!"

Iyanla Vanzant (pronounced E-Yan-La), a woman who has been hailed by many as one of the most influential African American women of our day, connected

with millions of households from 2004 to 2006 when
she served as a life coach on the television show *Starting
Over*. The purpose of this popular daytime drama was
to help women transform their lives by placing them in
a supportive environment—the *Starting Over* House—
where they could do just that. Cheering one another
on, buoyed by the guidance of three gifted coaches, the
women would "graduate" into sparkling new versions
of themselves. Iyanla, more than the other two mentors, subtly offered spiritual guidance, encouraging the
women to engage in soulful practices—silence, reflection,
and journaling—while cultivating love and compassion
for themselves.

When I speak with her in the fall in 2004, I ask her
why this show? Why now, after so many years of successful writing (a string of *New York Times* best sellers)
and international acclaim as a dynamic speaker? Iyanla
answers, "Because I know more than anybody, maybe,
how to start over. I've done it so many times in my life."
From childhood abandonment, through physical and
emotional abuse, to living on welfare, this powerhouse
of a woman knows what it means to be down and out
and, very practically, how to rise above it all and live life
to the fullest. Truly, who better to teach someone else
how to start over?

Iyanla shares with me how, in her late twenties, she
embarked on her first big "starting over": She put herself
through law school. One day, while riding a bus in New
York City, where she lived, a billboard on the side of
the road caught her attention. It said, "If you're ready
to change your life, come to college." "So I did!" she
laughs heartily. "And I took my kids with me. I went to
Medgar Evers College where 98 percent of the students

are African American. I received financial aid to go there. My kids would sit outside the door of my classroom and do their homework or play in the gym, or someone, usually a teacher, would take them in so I could study." Upon graduation, Iyanla became a legal advocate for the powerless. She has always had a special place in her heart for women who were struggling to come into their own, as she had.

"We all have many, many opportunities to start over," Iyanla explains. "When we come to that place where we can see that what we are doing is not in alignment with our desires, our authentic self, we have to stop and start over." That is something Iyanla continues to do even to the present day, for, as of this writing, she has started over once more. When the television show ended, she moved back to Maryland, rededicating herself to public speaking and working with the Inner Visions Institute of Spiritual Development, which she founded in 1998—a collaborative of holistic practitioners who motivate and inspire others to create a better life, a better community of humankind. Rarely, in all the years I have interviewed women, have I met someone with such fiery passion to live so firmly entrenched in the Spirit, in complete service to others, as Iyanla Vanzant.

I am so very grateful for her contagious zeal, for it raised me from the bowels of my own low point as my twenty-four-year marriage fell apart. Her book *In the Meantime: Finding Yourself and the Love You Want* was a humor-infused godsend. Its no-nonsense wisdom helped me cope with how to live "in the meantime"— that in-between place where you don't know how to stay in a relationship, don't know how to leave, and you just keep hoping that something good will come out of all the mess. Her book *Faith in the Valley: Lessons for Women on the Journey to Peace* was a further balm to my spirit during this challenging time in my life.

As we converse on the telephone, it's 7:00 a.m., and she's sitting in her apartment in Los Angeles. Even this early in the morning, she is bright and chipper, and we find ourselves turning to discuss, again and again, the source of her passion—New Thought principles. Ordained as a New Thought minister, Iyanla shares her foundational belief with me that we do, indeed, have the ability to choose our lives, no matter what our history, no matter our family of origin, no matter what tragedies have befallen us. We have the capability, through the power of choice, to become who we are destined to be— holy women. "Change comes from within," she says, "and until you decide 'Today is the day,' no amount of coaching from others will help."

Iyanla was not the first one to introduce me to these principles. She simply reminded me—and embodied in a bright enough female version for me to see—what had been intimated to me years earlier by my father and a book in our family library, *As a Man Thinketh* by British philosopher and poet, James Allen. (A more woman-friendly version has, thankfully, been translated for us by Dorothy Hulst.) "A woman is literally what she thinks—her character being the complete sum of her thoughts" is its core principle.[1] In other words, what we think about expands, creating our reality as we know it.

Over the years, these principles sank in, and I began to "play" with them, acutely noticing how what I read affected my thoughts and mood, as did the people I associated with and the conversations we shared. Television, movies, newspapers, all affected my thinking and how I felt. It became evident to me that what I turned toward for relief or entertainment had an end result, either positive or negative. That awareness brought empowerment and along with it a growing desire to be more proactive about my life. I desired more for myself. I wanted to think better, feel better.

So did Iyanla. Deep within her she had a knowing that she could, somehow, turn her life around—that she could become more than who she was at that particular moment in time. "For me," she relates, "it meant building a totally new foundation of life for myself, because my own beginnings were laid haphazardly, laid unlovingly, laid abusively. First of all, I had to tell the truth about my early experience, not coloring it, clouding it, or covering it over. Simply saying, 'This is what it is.' Then asking myself, 'Do I want more of this, or do I want something else?' I didn't want more physical abuse, verbal abuse, rejection, and betrayal. So I had to look at those ways that it had been done to me and also at the ways I had done it to myself as a function of how my early foundation had been laid. I began by telling the truth about myself."

Iyanla believes that each of us has the power to think, feel, and act in an entirely new way. One that is Spirit-infused, Spirit-led, *if we choose it to be.* She coined a two-word maxim for herself that helped her continue to make appropriate life choices and move into a greater experience of her "God-self," as she calls it. This phrase, "until today," would eventually become a book title, and the words she would use to urge any woman in the *Starting Over* House on to victory. "When someone parrots her history by claiming 'Well, I've *always* done it this way,' then I respond, 'Until today!'"

"Until today" is the mantra we can use when negativity or powerlessness rules our thinking; when life throws us curves and we begin to lose sight of the shores of our own glory or when the going gets tough. "Until today" means we no longer have to be who we have been.

Iyanla is firm on this. As we speak, I feel her energy rise like a cone of power, even over the telephone, as she describes the process she used to begin to reshape her life. "Journaling," she says emphatically. "It's the very best way I know to look at what you're thinking, what you're saying, how you're feeling, and what you're doing. Journaling is self-reflection, self-correction. That's what I had to do and what I think all women can benefit from. It helps us tell the truth and become aware. Then we can remake our lives. We can set a new intention, make a commitment to that intention, and invest our time and energy into making the changes we desire."

What Iyanla is referring to in her practice of self-reflection through journaling is learning how to be the "observer." The observer is the dispassionate watcher of our thoughts and feelings, the discerner of all that is going on in our mind. To observe we begin to adopt the mind of a scientist who desires to take something apart to better understand how it works and why. If we are the sum total of all our thoughts, as James Allen would say, it is vitally important for us to understand who we have become as a result of those thoughts and how our lives have been created—by others and by ourselves. Through being our own observer, we can take an honest look at the thoughts that continue to dominate our mindset.

On average, sixty thousand thoughts a day run through our minds. We can begin to observe—simply notice—the content of these thoughts and where they lead us emotionally. We can discern: Does their presence take me into a greater daily experience of Spirit? Toward inner peace, self-confidence, joy, and gratitude? Or do these thoughts keep me bound up in worry, self-doubt, fear, or lack? We can observe if our thoughts are Spirit-led or ego-dominated. Then, because we desire to live in a truly sacred manner, we must tell the truth about what we've discovered and pledge to redirect our thinking.

I ask Iyanla if she still continues to journal, to "house-clean," as she calls it, for the purpose of self-correction. "Not as much as I'd like," she admits, "because of my work schedule these days. But I mentally journal now. I have gotten really good at running it down in my mind, and then I have a delete button in my own head. I notice my thinking, and if it's not okay, I press delete. You're gone!" she laughs.

On the second occasion that I interview Iyanla, it is, again, 7:00 a.m., and she shares with me that even at this early hour she has already begun her day by engaging in practices that keep her thoughts and feelings focused on the positive. "I have a three-inch-deep three-ring binder, and in it I have things I have found over the years: prayers, affirmations, techniques, pages out of books, sayings that I want to keep. I go through that book every morning and program my mind. I don't wait until noon or for when I get upset. When my feet hit the floor, before the coffee, before the TV, I program my mind. My house is silent right now, and I've been programming myself."

Another dynamic daily practice that helps Iyanla stay rooted in positive thoughts and Spirit is her "I Am" book. "You see, 'I Am' is the creative energy of God," she explains, "so whatever you attach 'I Am' to you must become, because that is the creative energy in which we are sourced. I start my day with three pages of 'I Am' statements." She begins to recite them for me, and, as she does, I can feel her energy quicken. The timbre of her voice rises, and an excitement builds that spills over into me as well.

"I am doing the will and work of God," she chants. "I am creating positive and powerful transformation as I facilitate and support the personal growth and healing of women throughout the world. I am honoring truth. I am allowing myself to be seen. I am allowing myself to be heard. I am trusting myself to know what to do and say at all times. . . ."

And on she goes. As she moves through her list, her voice carries me to a far off place where I experience her in my mind's eye as priestess, arms to the sky, beckoning the women seated in the circle around her to welcome in their own "I Am" presence. The drums beat and spirits soar on the wings of song up to the heavens. Later in our conversation, I learn that Iyanla is, truly, a Yoruba priestess, "dedicated to honor, uphold, and promote the spiritual philosophy and culture of the Yoruba people." My image of her, majestically attuned to the Spirit and the spirit of her people on Africa's shores, is, uncannily, not far from the truth.

Iyanla creates her "I Am" list, she tells me, by taking an honest look at all the things in her life she hasn't done or the things she's afraid to do. Then she turns each one into a powerful "I Am" statement. This indicates to me that she is being the ultimate observer and the cocreator of her life. She believes her life—each of our lives—is a cocreative effort between ourselves and the Divine. It is up to us to choose our thoughts and change our behavior.

A cocreative life is one that is consciously created by us with assistance from our Source. The Divine will lend its support and guidance as we do so.

"As human beings, as noble and divine and creative as we are, we can't do it alone. You have to have a connection to your Higher Self—your God-self—and to the God of your understanding. There are some things only grace can heal. Some things only grace can do. I call God Grace On Demand. And I'm glad it's 'Grace' and not 'George!' It's still a feminine energy," Iyanla laughs. "This is the Presence as I understand it, *my* Presence."

The invitation here is to begin to live in *alignment*, a term Iyanla has used often throughout our conversation. Alignment is a state of being whereby our thoughts, words, and actions are "in sync," each one in harmony with the other. Each builds upon the other to take us into an embodied experience of our truest self—or not.

For example, she explains, if we say we love others but speak badly or gossip about them, we are not in alignment. Our thoughts and feelings do not match our actions. In fact, they are a contradiction. If we say that we desire peace in the world but have feelings of anger, bitterness, or resentment toward others, we are not walking our talk. We are not in alignment.

We change this, and change ourselves, by doing what Iyanla so passionately espouses. We notice the nature of our thoughts, then consciously choose only those that bring us into alignment with our highest desires—rather than align with those of our false, ego self. This powerful process is one of the highest forms of spiritual practice we can engage in.

Author Dorothy Hulst presents it to us this way: "Woman is made or unmade by herself; in the armory of her thoughts she destroys herself; she also fashions the tools with which she builds for herself heavenly mansions of joy and strength and peace."[2] Some of Iyanla's tools are a three-ring binder full of inspiration, a list of "I Am" affirmations, and daily journaling. Each of us must craft our own tools and use them faithfully. (We will be crafting tools and practices like these for ourselves in the following chapters.)

To begin to track our thoughts, words, and actions as Iyanla has, however, requires one very important skill, one that was introduced here in "I Am Free to Live a Spiritual Life of My Own Making" (pages 17–33)—the ability to access silence. It is absolutely impossible to get in touch with our thoughts and feelings if we cannot sit still enough to listen. For that very reason, periods of silence-infused solitude are vital to our spiritual journey.

Yet many women over the years have told me that they absolutely cannot get quiet; silence eludes them. They have tried meditation, and it doesn't work. Even prayer is full of mind chatter. A very simple practice of *noticing our thinking*, in time, can change all that. Buddhist teacher Pema Chödrön can be our guide here. She advises us to begin by sitting down and accessing as much quiet as we can. (Even if there is very little initially, that's all right. We begin anyway.) Then we watch our thoughts just float on through our mind. We simply notice them and observe how they take us somewhere else. Next, we label those distracting thoughts as "thinking."[3] By acknowledging them in this way—even saying the word "thinking" to ourselves when we notice their presence—we find ourselves not being lured away quite so often.

If we desire to live in a sacred manner, we must begin to clear out mind clutter and create room for peace, love, and joy to dwell. Taking up mental gardening is a wonderful (and gentle) metaphor for reclaiming our thoughts in this way. "A woman's mind may be likened to a garden," translates Dorothy Hulst, "which may be intelligently cultivated or allowed to run wild. . . . Just as a gardener cultivates her plot, keeping it free from weeds, and growing the flowers and fruits which she requires, so may a woman tend the garden of her mind. . . . By pursuing this process, a woman sooner or later discovers that she is the master-gardener of her soul, the director of her life."[4]

We engage in this mental gardening process lovingly, patiently. Eliminating weed thoughts and selectively sowing seeds that will produce thoughts, feelings, and actions of peace and joy. We are gentle with ourselves as we unlearn old ways of thinking and master new, more beneficial ones.

It is not only our thoughts that we reorient toward the Spirit, but our emotions as well—though some may doubt this could even be possible. Emotions feel wild and volatile. They can catch us off guard and whisk us into a realm of discomfort or conflict in the blink of an eye. Like thoughts, feelings can, with observation and intentional practice, be diffused and redirected. Negative emotions, especially those touted by the ego—anger, worry, disappointment, distrust, and conflict—take us far away from our divine identity.

We can begin to "work" with them just like we do our thoughts. For example, when a strong emotion comes up, we can hold it. We give it time. We wait for it to lessen, even dissipate. Mind-body scientist Dr. Jon Kabat-Zinn writes of this powerful process in his book *Coming to Our Senses*. When we find ourselves in a rage or some other strong (negative) emotion, we can do what we would at a railroad crossing: "Stop, look, listen. Ask yourself, 'Right now, what's happening?' Your response might be, 'I'm completely flipped out, or confused, or terrified.' But then you can say, 'Fine, let's wait. Let's not try to fix it, deny it, make it go away, or pursue it.' Just allow your awareness to hold it."[5]

Dr. Zinn goes on to say that if we can embrace anger, for instance, if we are able to just watch what happens, the emotion will rise to a peak, then begin to dissolve. We can actually learn how to surf the anger (or any other strong emotion) and have it not lead us into some action or statement we are going to regret. With time and continued practice, we will learn to relate to our emotions differently. They do not have to drag us, like an out-of-control dog on a leash, down the road of our mind—away from our God-self.

Of all the practices I have engaged in that take me deeper into my truest self, this may be the most powerful. For my entire life I have been a highly sensitive woman whose strong emotions can predominate. They can rise in a nanosecond, taking me from calm to chaos. Through an intentional practice, not unlike what Dr. Zinn describes, I have become a better surfer of my emotions.

When I feel a strong emotion come up, I experience it in one of two places in my body—my gut or my heart. Within seconds of the emotion rising, I take a deep breath and bring my attention to it. I feel it, but quickly shift, as best I can, to observer mode. I hold the feeling within me in silence, then I give it a name. "Anger."

"Impatience." "Irritation." Whatever the emotion might be, by noticing it and naming it, I have begun to have a different relationship with it. Now the emotion is only something I am experiencing. It is not *me*. I am not an angry, impatient, or irritable person. Those qualities are something I might occasionally experience, but that is all they are—pure experience. I can choose, in most instances, not to act upon them. The process of naming the emotion is truly transformative. It allows us to buy some time so the disconnect from its influence can begin. Naming it enables us to engage with the emotion in a completely different way.

Sometimes humor is helpful, too, in dealing with the ego and its negative feelings. My favorite method? When a nasty emotion comes to call, I address the feeling like a surprise visitor. I imagine the emotion as a pesky green gnome—an annoying little bugger who jumps up and down next to me to get my attention. When the emotion surfaces, I stop, look, and acknowledge that he's there. I thank him for coming to visit and then add, "No thanks. I don't think I want to spend any time with you right now." Usually, within a few minutes and a few deep breaths, my ego visitor has faded into the ether. I think Iyanla, though I never shared it with her, would appreciate this technique. My "no thanks" is very much like her "until today."

You may recall that women in Holy Orders took vows (and many still do) that are designed to help them align themselves with the Divine: chastity, poverty, obedience, and humility. I believe that the holy women of today— you and me—are being invited to take a new vow, and Iyanla is our mother superior who can show us how. It is the "Vow of Transparency."

To be transparent, as Iyanla is, means that we are passionate enough about our own healing journey to look at ourselves openly and honestly. We acknowledge our history and the stories we keep telling about ourselves. Transparency means there is no more hiding from ourselves, from others, and most importantly, from our Source.

Taking a vow of transparency indicates that we are willing to make space within ourselves and clear out from our body temple "the emotional debris of a lifetime . . ." as Thomas Keating describes it. "We become closer to God because, through the process of unloading, we have evacuated some of the material that was hiding the divine Presence."[6]

Bearing witness to the life expression of Iyanla Vanzant, we see that her passion and purpose is to do just this. She invites us to be the highest expression of our God-self in the world that we can be by embodying the third Transformational Truth:

I Choose Thoughts and Feelings That Honor My Sacred Self

As my conversation with Iyanla draws to a close, I pose one final question to her—the same question I've asked each of the luminaries I've interviewed. What might she be personally struggling with now at this point in her pilgrimage? I've done so, not out of intrusive curiosity, but because I am eager to know what it is that still challenges each woman, regardless of her level of illumination. And so I ask it of Iyanla, not knowing what I will hear.

Her response is silence. I wait. In soft, thoughtful tones she haltingly reveals, "In December I buried my thirty-one-year-old daughter." I am stunned by her answer and for a fleeting moment embarrassed that I've asked such a deeply personal question, especially one that elicited such an agonizing response. "I don't understand why she had to die," she continues. "She was conscious, and she was awake. She was the most gentle, loving person alive, and we traveled together for years, she and I, and her daughter, and a dear friend. We called ourselves 'Three Women and a Baby.' No one ever said an ill word about her. She always had a smile on her face. Anytime you were in need, she was there."

I learn that this tragic loss was a pivotal reason Iyanla agreed to do the *Starting Over* show—why she left family and friends behind on the East Coast to move to Los Angeles all by herself. "It forced me to stop grieving. I was in bed for months, it seemed, stuck in the fetal position. I couldn't move, couldn't think. If I'd stayed home, people would have encouraged me to grieve more because they were all grieving, too. I still mourn, but now I get up every morning and go to work."

And then, like before, I feel her energy rise, as if she has plugged in to a life-giving Source. Powerful positivity slowly returns. "You know," she adds, "if I could be with my daughter, I'd leave here today, but I don't know if I would recognize her. That would mean I'd have to leave the party here and what if I never found her, my ultimate date?"

Oh, Iyanla, I think to myself as I hang up the telephone, what an inspiration you are to all of us! You really were "starting over" when you appeared on television each day, and none of us even knew it. As we watched you reach out to others and inspire them to be the best they could be, *you* were struggling to keep going, healing from the most horrible wound any of us can imagine— the loss of a child—in the only way you knew how. You took a long loving look at what was real and made a new choice for yourself, then reached out to help others do the same. You are, indeed, the queen of commitment to embodying your truest self in God.

As we continue to make new choices for ourselves as Iyanla has, choices that bring us into greater alignment with our most sacred selves, may we do so with patience and gentleness. We need not be spiritual warriors to reclaim ourselves as holy and whole. Let us grant ourselves all the time we need to lovingly release habituated ways. May we bestow tender, loving care upon ourselves as we assimilate new ways of being.

"A new moon teaches gradualness and deliberation," wrote Rumi, "and how one gives birth to oneself slowly. Patience with small details makes perfect a large work, like the universe."

Like the universe within ourselves.

Reflection Questions

1. Are you aware of the ways in which your external environment (settings, people, events) affect your thoughts and feelings? Name some of those ways.
2. Do you believe you can choose how to respond to your thoughts and feelings? If so, how have you done so in the past?
3. What practices do you engage in daily to align your thoughts and feelings with the Divine (rather than the false self or ego)?

Peaceful Pause

Clearing the Mind

Close your eyes and sit quietly. Connect with the rhythm of your breath, noticing its gentle movement in and out. Focus your attention on this wonderful Spirit-filled breath. Feel your breath naturally calming you, slowing down mental busyness, bringing you into a place of peace.

Continuing to sit quietly, notice how your thoughts naturally drift off to focus on other things. That is all right. It is an automatic response of the mind to do so. When you observe that your thoughts have wandered off, gently bring your attention back to your breath. Refocus on the experience of breathing—in and out, in and out. Each time your mind wanders, repeat the process. Simply notice that it has drifted away, hold no opinion about that fact, and refocus on the breath.

When thoughts arise, taking you into arenas of worry or concern, replaying past events or jumping forward into the future, say these words silently to yourself:

> I notice these thoughts and feelings. They are only something I am temporarily experiencing. They are not me, nor my essence. I have the ability to set them aside and return to my quiet center—the place where I am at peace—at home—where the Sacred One lives and breathes within me.

truth
four

I Engage in Daily Practices
That Nurture My Spirit

Dudley Evenson

What nine months of attention does for an
  embryo,
forty early mornings will do
for your gradually growing wholeness.

Jalaluddin Rumi

It was their physical appearance, straight out of the 1960s, that caught my attention. As their company of long-haired musicians, colorfully dressed in flowing garb, took the stage, I couldn't help but be drawn back in time to a bygone time—one of passionate ideals of living together in peace, love, and harmony. Dean and Dudley Evenson, self admitted Flower Children and now sixty something adults, lifted their instruments and began to play a tune from their newest ambient music album. The room filled with the soulful strains of flute and harp, and within seconds I was transported to an inner space where peace reigned supreme.

After the concert, I wished I could meet them and thank them for the gift of their music. I was in awe of the power of the notes they played to transform and uplift. I had a deeper knowing, though, that their offering of peace through music wasn't due just to their consummate playing skills. The peace was sourced in the musicians themselves. It lived in their hearts and minds, flowed through their lips and hands like a river spills into the ocean. Dean and Dudley Evenson swam in a pool of inner peace, and when they played music, its soothing waters rippled out, bathing all of us in peace as well.

I never did get to meet the Evensons at the metaphysical trade show in Denver in 1997, but I did bring their music home with me. Over the years, their melodies— unique blends of earth rhythms, nature sounds, and soft chant—were the soothing backdrop for my writing. I thought of them often and wondered about their lifestyle: What choices might they make to stay rooted in the peace they conveyed through their music? It was not until seven years later that I was able to ask them myself.

It was time for the Holiday 2004 issue of the *Healing Garden Journal,* and as its editor, I was seeking someone to interview about the theme "peace and harmony." Who better than the Evensons? A quick phone call to their music company, Soundings of the Planet, resulted in a thought-provoking interview that would provide me with a new understanding of what it means to live a life firmly rooted in the Spirit.

As we spoke that day, one particular chord kept reverberating. No matter where we drifted in conversation, a refrain of peace permeated everything. In the tone of their voices, in their musings on the past, around their intentions for the future, peace prevailed. I could literally feel it. Just speaking with them made me feel more peaceful. It was obvious to me that no separation existed between their ideals, the way in which they made their living, and how they related to others. They were a complete expression of the byline of their award-winning record label—"Peace through Music." They *were* peace.

The interview I did with them was well received by our readers, and as the outline for this book came together, I naturally thought of Dudley as one of the women who should be featured in it. I remember well the day of our first private and lengthy conversation— the one where I asked her to tell me her story. There she was in her breezy home office overlooking a wild river in the foothills of the Cascade Mountains in Washington. I, on the other hand, was sequestered in my sweltering attic office in an old Victorian house on a busy street in northern Michigan. We spoke effortlessly for nearly two hours, as if we'd known each other for years. Time became nonexistent as I listened to her fascinating tale of love, passionate ideals, and a hippie bus—the stuff of which movies are made.

Dudley begins by telling me about her traditional Presbyterian upbringing. She was disappointed early on with how the people in church would say one thing and do another. "I tended to be very idealistic, loved the stories in the Bible, the teachings of Christ, so the hypocrisy that seemed prevalent always concerned me."

She was not the only one who observed her idealism. "My mother always told me, 'Dudley, you're too idealistic. You know you are going to be disappointed. The world isn't that way, and you'll be hurt.' I know she was trying to protect me, but I believe she didn't know that you can be idealistic and have hope and powerful beliefs in positive, loving possibilities."

It was this idealism and a vision of what could be that brought Dudley and Dean together in 1968. "I found in him," she says, "someone who was equally, if not more, idealistic than myself." They met when Dean moved to New York's East Village arts district. Dudley Dickinson,

who would soon become Dean's wife and artistic partner, was a photographer. Dean was a musician and a
scientist, working as a recording engineer at a sound
studio. Both were on a quest for spiritual knowledge and
a lifestyle rooted in the core values of the peace and love
movement of the times. They joined energies and took
off in a converted school bus to explore documentary
filmmaking. They soon found themselves engaged in
and filming some of the defining social and cultural
moments of the '70s and '80s, including the siege and
occupation of Wounded Knee in 1973 and the first
United Nations Conference on the Human Environment
in Stockholm, Sweden, in 1972.

Because living in peace with others in sustainable
harmony with Mother Nature was one of their youthful
ideals, the Evensons were drawn to communal living and
did so several times with varying groups of people. "We
had big gardens," Dudley explains, "and at one point
we were running a vegetarian restaurant in Woodstock,
New York, called the Rainbow Café." Later, they headed
to Florida on their bus, finding new people to live with.
"We had our second child in that bus. We let go of most
of our material needs and did a lot of bartering and
trading. We ground our own flour and made our own
flatbread."

She paints a vivid picture for me of going where life
took them, two free-spirited beings, living their ideals.
I recall her bright laugh as she describes this nomadic
life. "We called this our decade of intentional poverty,"
she chuckles. "It was just a wonderful, refreshing time,
and it was also a time of clarifying our vision and raising
our little girls. I treasure those times because we learned

so much about how to live lightly on the Earth and in harmony with others."

After many years of living a life on the road, in one commune after another, and three children later, the Evensons realized it was time to settle down. They got off the bus and purchased a house in Arizona. During their travels, they had become increasingly aware that though they were enjoying their lives for the most part, their dream was not yet complete. They wanted to do more with their music, make a real living at it, and make contributions to the world through it. So in 1979, Dean and Dudley founded their music company, Soundings of the Planet. Twenty-eight years later, the Evensons continue to be "keepers of the vision," now for a new generation of seekers who believe, as they do, that global peace and love can become a reality. And music, they believe, may just be one of the most powerful ways to make that happen.

As we speak I am curious to learn about Dudley's spiritual practices, as I am actively seeking my own. I know that if you meditate, pray, or engage in a practice like yoga faithfully, it can reshape you—make you more peaceful or kind—and I do want more of that. I wonder what she does each day to keep herself rooted in a peaceful mindset, so I ask her.

"Before I even get out of bed, I do a set of eye and breathing exercises," she explains. "Part of that includes fifty tummy rubs in each direction, along with eye squinting and rapid breathing. Then I raise my arms and offer a prayer of gratitude for all my blessings and ask that I may be guided to be used in the highest possible way during the day to help heal this world. I try to do a yoga routine and more breathing exercises and sit quietly to clear my mind and uplift my spirit. If the weather permits, I do this outside facing the morning sun. In the afternoon, I try to work in my garden or go for a two-mile walk along the river where I live."

She shares how she and Dean continue with their peace-filled practices throughout the evening. "After dinner, we often play music together. We chant or tone [for healing]. Before going to bed, we may sit quietly and meditate. Sometimes we enjoy our hot tub out under the stars."

As I visualize her doing these things, I realize that her entire day is full of peaceful practices—from first waking until bedtime. I imagine what discipline it must take to be so dedicated. Suddenly, out of the blue, a realization comes, and I see that I've had it all backward—this understanding of how one arrives at authentic spiritual practices.

I've been holding on to a false notion that we must search to find them. How, with time and dedication, we will locate the right ones, then, by staying faithful to them, we'll become "more spiritual." Instead, an awareness begins to take shape that the ideals and core values we hold dear must come first—that our personal practices will organically emerge from those ideals. I realize that Dudley is the perfect example of how this process works.

If we look carefully beneath the surface of her spiritual practices, we see Dudley's core values at work in both her morning and evening routine: health and well-being, gratitude, service to others, connection with the Earth, relating harmoniously to others, creative self-expression, and more. The thread of inner peace runs throughout.

Inner peace and harmony with others is the foundation of her day.

Dudley's spiritual practices have emerged as a result of being highly attuned to her core values—values that originated in childhood, took root in college, and came to full fruition in adulthood.

If this is how it is, how do any of us come to discover our own spiritual practices? We can begin as Dudley did, with getting in touch with our core values—by determining what it is we wish our lives to represent. Is it inner peace, love, health and well-being, gratitude? Whatever our particular ideal is, we can hold it close to our heart so that when an opportunity comes to engage in a new activity (or practice) we can measure it against that. Our ideals can be the measuring stick by which we gauge if a particular activity or action is right and true for us.

Next, we keep our hearts and minds open, our bodies attuned, to *feel* if it affirms the ideals we espouse.

For example, for many years I spent my first hour upon waking with the radio or television. I felt I needed the news to energize me, to stay in touch with what was happening in the world. In time, I began to notice that this morning news routine was having a depressive effect on me. I experienced it most acutely during the coverage of the Oklahoma City bombing in 1995. I recall how anguished I was over the horror of this event, and how I sat, hour after hour, for nearly three days, frozen in front of the television. I could not seem to break away from the painful images. They pulled me into their clutches like a magnet.

I finally made the connection, thankfully, realizing that these less-than-wonderful feelings diminished the quality of my day. My deep desire to greet the day joy-fully was of ultimate importance, and from that moment on, I chose to start my day with activities that would enliven me: gentle music, a walk in nature, sitting in silence, reading something inspirational. I chose daily spiritual practices that allow me to begin and move through my day rooted in my core values—inner peace and happiness.

By using our core values as a measuring stick, we can organically feel, and begin to gather to us, the daily spiritual practices that provide sustenance. We can give ourselves permission to explore various practices, try them on for size, listen for our body's response, and self-assess. We then make an honest determination: Is this practice moving us toward wholeness and the Spirit? Or does the practice appeal to our ego-based thinking, especially those nasty "shoulds"? The ego may also draw us toward certain practices out of its base need for recognition, vanity, or even spiritual superiority. We need to ask ourselves: Does this practice align me with the core values I wish my life to represent?

Our challenge is to find the practices, as Dudley has, that do exactly that. The list of spiritual practices one can explore is endless. There are quiet practices: various forms of prayer, meditation, silence, or sacred reading; active practices: singing, chanting, dancing, worship, or creative expression; and physical practices: yoga, bowing, tai chi, gardening, or mindful walking. Spiritual practices can be done alone or with others. In one's home, in nature, in a church, temple, or mosque, at all times of day or night.

The variety of spiritual practices is boundless, as are our perceptions and understandings of the Divine. My friend Pam's daily spiritual practice is a mindful walk in the woods. This is how she connects with God—through nature. Julie has a centering prayer group. She experiences the Spirit most deeply with others in community. Barb dances. For her, God is one of limitless expression and movement. Laurie kayaks. Marilyn says the rosary. Sherrie gardens.

A spiritual practice done consistently will bring us to a greater daily experience of Spirit. The practice itself creates sacred space within us—room for the Divine to be made manifest. Philanthropist Tara Guber, founder of the Yoga House in California, describes her particular spiritual practice—meditation—as "taking time in."[1] Indeed, this is what any spiritual practice does. It pulls us from the outside in, from the world at large back into our inner world—into our sacred self—the place where peace, love, and joy naturally reside.

Brother Wayne Teasdale, a Catholic monk with Eastern leanings, devoted much of his life to understanding the nature of spiritual practice. He reminded us that worldly distractions can keep us from spiritual matters. If we desire to be Spirit-filled people, "We have to pay more attention to God, which translates practically into putting more time each day into our spiritual life."[2] In his book *The Mystic Heart*, he often refers to spiritual practice as spiritual discipline. It is a discipline because our chosen practice requires time and energy. It demands a strong commitment, fueled by passion, to pull ourselves away from the distractions and busyness of our physical world.

It takes time for a spiritual practice to work its magic upon us—to root us more deeply in the Spirit. It takes perhaps even more time for the ego and its pull to soften. With dedication, the lines of distinction will blur between ourselves and the practice. Its results—inner calm, openheartedness, generosity of spirit—begin to melt into us. One day we may actually awaken to realize that we not only *feel* more loving, but we have *become* more loving; that we do not just *feel* more peaceful, but we have *become* a peaceful presence in the world. I sense that this is precisely what happened with Dudley, and the key to her embodiment is dailiness. Spiritual practice, done faithfully, does grow the spiritual life. And it grows us.

Spiritual practice is "the heart of our spiritual life," said Br. Teasdale. "Spiritual practice is to the mystical life what food and water are to the body. . . . They are the inner source of nourishment and growth."[3] Yes, sublime comfort can be found in spiritual practice. Again, this is what I sense with Dudley. The practices she describes for me are so gentle, completely nourishing her. They are that special "something" she can rely on each time to bring her home to her truest self, to the Divine. The practice itself can also become a dear friend and traveling companion.

She shares with me how much she and Dean travel, playing their music for others. Her spiritual practices, thankfully, can travel right along with her. They dependably deliver her to the shores of peace and harmonious relations with others no matter where she finds herself geographically.

Our spiritual practice can be a soft place to fall into the arms of God wherever we are, whenever life feels uncomfortable or challenging. The mat, the prayer rug, the temple, the pew, the home altar, the woods, or the shore—each can provide the sacred space we desire.

For many years, Dudley has been an outspoken proponent for music as a spiritual practice. It provides not only comfort and nourishment, but can actually heal us. Dudley herself is living proof. During a particularly challenging period in her life, she put this core belief of hers to work for self-healing. She literally "sang herself well."

She had begun to experience hearing loss in her right ear. She thought this might be due to many stressful hours on the telephone trying to work out nagging problems within their business. "Then one day I woke up and the room was spinning," she tells me. "I got dizzy and threw up. I had frightening attacks like this along with hearing loss." A medical exam revealed nothing. Ever the believer that our body and emotions are connected, Dudley began to evaluate what her responsibility might be in all this. What might she be doing on a mental and emotional level to contribute to this disorder? "I looked at a number of things," she shares, "and so I asked myself, 'Am I working too hard? Do I need to eat better? Am I joyful? Am I singing every day?'"

In a moment of illumination, she realized she was not singing at all, something she loved to do very much. She was too busy working, was overly stressed, and it was affecting her health. She decided to create a healing ritual to help her reclaim her peace of mind and body. "I innately knew I needed to clear myself of any judgments, any conflicts that I had with others, and just open up my mind and heart. What I did was create a little melody. I would go for walks in the woods and just sing, thankful for the trees, the sky, the birds. I just opened my heart and sang."

I ask Dudley if she will sing it for me and she does in a beautiful, lyrical voice. "Clear my mind . . . open my heart . . . heal my body . . . heal my world." As she repeats it, I see her in my mind's eye, long, dark hair flowing in the breeze, meandering through the woods like an enraptured child, singing herself well. Listening to her healing mantra, my heart expands along with the melody.

Within ten days of beginning this practice, Dudley says her dizziness and nausea stopped. Within months, her hearing was greatly restored. She believes she was able to shift her molecular structure, through her intentions, her mental focus, and by physically singing.

"It's not an accident that singing hymns and chanting is all part of spiritual practice. What they do is bring spiritual thoughts and principles into the physical through our voice and heart. It allows them to be experienced through our bodies. Such practices can actually open the heart and heal the body," Dudley says. She tells me she still uses her healing mantra whenever it is needed. Chanting it, along with time spent in nature, reconnects her with her truest self.

Any spiritual practice to which we fully commit— body, mind, and heart—will inevitably change us, often in surprising ways. The discipline of returning to it, surrendering to it, will teach us what we still need to know about ourselves. In meditation—what hooks us into busy thinking. In fasting—how addicted we are to food. In dancing—how self-conscious we are. In prayer—how much we avoid spending time with the Divine. Anything we are invited to return to again and again—like spiritual practice—will reveal where we resist or hold back, where we are dominated by our ego rather than our spirit—what we need to let go of, have faith in, or trust.

We should also not be surprised if, at some point in our pilgrimage, our once-beloved spiritual practice begins to bring discomfort or dissatisfaction. If in meditation we get restless, or we find ourselves bored with centering prayer, we are likely being given an indicator of where we still need to grow. The practice itself can help us break through habitual ways of responding to life; to run away when things become difficult; to go on to the next electrifying thing that promises immediate gratification. Paying attention to what the practice brings up invites us to live with openness, with expansiveness, not so much toward others, but toward ourselves. Long-term dedication to a spiritual practice births the courage and compassion we need to accept ourselves as we are right now.

And if, by chance or life circumstance, we fall away from our spiritual practices, what then? We treat ourselves gently, for that in itself is a spiritual practice—compassion. Cultivating patience can also be a form of spiritual practice. Doing so allows us to begin again. We return once more to the mat, the woods, the canvas, or the pew and allow it to teach us, enlighten us about ourselves.

With time and persistence, a spiritual practice can actually become a form of prayer for us. Simone Weil, the French philosopher and mystic, once said, "Prayer is paying complete attention to something." I learn that Dudley has found this to be true for herself. "When I first began to explore meditation and yoga years ago, I remember noticing at one point that I was putting my body into positions of prayer. It just wasn't being on my knees, but stretching and reaching out and humbling myself. I found myself honoring my body as a temple, a house for my soul."

Music, for Dudley, has also been a form of passionate prayer, a true offering of herself and her gifts to the Spirit for use in the world. Music is her unique way of communicating with the Divine. Whether she is composing, singing, or playing, music is her primary form of spiritual practice. "Music connects us on a deep, visceral level to the soul," she states.

In looking at the totality of her life, we see there is no difference between the practices Dudley has cultivated and the bright being she is. Peace is her core value, her daily life, and the expression she offers back to the world. As a result, she fully embodies her spiritual values. "I don't know how many lives we have to live," she says, "but we have one life, right here, right now. It's important for each person to figure out how to balance their own spiritual yearnings with the realities of life—how to earn a living, their relationship with their family, and so on. It is important to modify the life we are given and cocreate it with our Creator in our own, unique way." Dudley Evenson invites us, just as she has, to integrate the fourth Transformational Truth into our lives:

I Engage in Daily Practices That Nurture My Spirit

Dudley is continually seeking new ways of expressing her core values of peace and harmonious living to others. Perhaps this is what I admire about her the most. Her tirelessness, her passionate dedication to serving others, even at an age when most Baby Boomers, like herself, are retiring. It seems the Evensons are on the road again, this time not in an old-school bus, but flying from city to city, meeting with veterans of the Iraq war. I learn that they have created a DVD called *Eagle River* to help returning soldiers heal from posttraumatic stress disorder (PTSD). They have blended their trademark relaxing music with stunning videography and guided meditations led by Dudley to help soldiers relax and heal. This news touches me in a profound way, because my oldest daughter is an ex-Marine who has served twice in Iraq. She is suffering from PTSD herself.

Today, when I think about the Evensons and their selfless service to others, I am filled with gratitude. My heart swells, my mind fills with the refrains of a John Lennon tune, "Imagine," which they have re-recorded on their own album, "Imagine Peace." They truly are the dreamers of which Lennon sings.

For the last forty years, Dean and Dudley have been holding a vision for all of us of a world where peace and love prevail. And they are still reaching out to others to make that dream a reality, this time to a new generation of young people with whom they share their message of healing and hope. By the example of their lives, they've issued a powerful invitation for us to join them. It is my hope and prayer that we will accept their invitation and rededicate ourselves to "Being the peace," as Gandhi would say, in a world that desperately needs our peaceful, loving presence.

Reflection Questions

1. What would you say are your core values in relation to your spiritual life?
2. Are you engaging in spiritual practices that reflect those core values? If so, what are they? How has doing them enhanced your life?
3. Is there anything in your life that prevents you from enjoying regular spiritual practice? What could you do to remove these obstacles?

Peaceful Pause

Inner Guidance

Bring your attention to the center of your chest. Imagine a translucent star there, glowing ever so softly as you focus on it. You notice that it can vary in brightness, glowing more brightly or gently fading, much like a pulsating heart.

As you engage in any spiritual practice of your choosing, take a moment to notice how brightly your star heart is glowing. Notice if engaging in that particular practice causes it to glow more brightly, remain constant, or to dim. Use this star as a guidepost to discern if your chosen spiritual practice is sustaining your spirit or not.

Repeat to yourself the following intention:

> I trust that the star in my heart will lead me to the spiritual practices that take me deeper into the heart of the Divine. I trust its luminosity to serve as a bright beacon for me, guiding me into greater daily experiences of peace, love, and happiness.

truth
five

I Cultivate Compassion
for Myself

Sue Patton Thoele

The whole world changes when we honor our-
selves. We gentle it. The fruit of self-knowledge
is kindness.

Joan Chittister, O.S.B.

"Wonderful Weirdness," she calls it, that serendipi-
tous aligning of spiritual forces that bring you
what you need just when you need it the most. More
times than I can count, Sue Patton Thoele has been my
Wonderful Weirdness companion. The first time was
through her book *The Courage to Be Yourself*. Just as I was
beginning to doubt the validity of my spiritual journey,
there she was, filled with good humor and wisdom,
assuring me that I was, indeed, on the right road to
uncovering my truest self.

Sue's book, now a classic guide to overcoming emotional dependence, is her personal tale of recovery, told
with stunning transparency. The passage that lured me
in was a candid confession of her own tendency to feel
responsible for the lives of everyone around her. Oh,
how familiar that sounded! "I'd convinced myself,"
she wrote, "that my clients couldn't make it without
me, and that my family needed my constant support,
ever-wise counsel, and ready sense of humor. I was
indispensable!"

Sue describes how, one day, she found herself sick, flat on her back, unable to take care of anyone, much less herself. Me, too, I thought. Been there, done that. Though Sue's illness was temporary—ten days straight—mine had lasted for years. A string of stress-related illnesses kept me ailing for over a decade, many of those years a blur of frustration and physical and mental exhaustion. Like Sue, I wanted to be all that I could be to my husband, three children, my clients and coworkers, my friends, and my extended family. But it was all too much.

Sue, like myself, had ignored the red flags of physical ailments, stress, resentment, and anger that waved wildly to get her attention. Despite their alert, she continued to don her Wonder Woman costume when someone had a need. "Surprise!" said Sue:

> Wonder Woman finally fell into bed and stayed there. . . . The fear that led me to get sick was that if I didn't give my all, always, I wouldn't be good enough, and if I weren't good enough, surely I would be unloved and abandoned. Clients would leave, children would feel neglected, husband would be disappointed—oh, horrors! I wouldn't be *perfect!* It took illness to show me that I'd reverted to two old patterns familiar to many women: 1) taking care of everyone else first; and 2) being perfect in order to be okay.[1]

What struck a deep chord of appreciation within me was Sue's unique ability to take on a serious subject— emotional dependence—with lightness of heart and humor. I'd had enough seriousness to last me a lifetime; I was more than ready to take myself and life more lightly! So in 1995, I adopted Sue as my recovery coach, primarily through her many books. Like a worldly wise older sister, I hung on every word, especially her "daily books"—*The Woman's Book of Courage* and *The Woman's Book of Confidence*. They bolstered me like no others when I had a bad attack of wimpiness about not being able "to do it all," or guilt when I'd taken time out to be good to myself.

It was not until I authored my own book years later on women's body, mind, and spirit wellness (*Coming Home to Ourselves*) that I was able to finally meet her. It was at the same trade show in Denver in 1997 where I saw the Evensons. Sue was a featured guest author with whom attendees could have a dialogue-based lunch. Of course, I jumped at the chance. As providence would have it, the hordes of people I thought would show up didn't, and I found myself sitting right next to her at a cozy table of eight women. Wonderful Weirdness!

She was nothing like I thought she would be. She'd proclaimed herself in her writing as "a Buddheo-Christian-Sufi-Experiential Mystic with plans to expand." A true New-Age woman. To me, she looked more like a sturdy Midwestern grandmother with permed hair and practical shoes. She was so very *ordinary*, and because of that I loved her immediately. At lunch that day, her genuine warmth enfolded us all in a cocoon of gentleness and self-acceptance, and we chatted for a good two hours about—truthfully—I don't remember what. Nevertheless, my fate with her was sealed that day. Sue Patton Thoele became my dearest mentor for life.

The rest, as they say, is history. Within a year, she had agreed to write the foreword to the next edition of my book, and our friendship blossomed via e-mail, cards,

and telephone conversations. When the time came to
write this book, she was, of course, the very first woman
I thought to include. Her motto, for which she had
become known, *"Live gently with yourself and others,"* had
become my pathway to wholeness, and I was eager to
share her, and it, with others.

As we journey more deeply into our truest selves,
we may wonder how it is that anyone can *really* live
more gently with themselves—in a practical manner,
that is—considering the demanding pace of our lives.
The answer to this question may be best answered by a
poem, one Sue wrote years ago. It was eventually made
into a poster, she tells me, with its own brief claim to
fame. Daphne, a main character on the television sitcom
Frasier, had it hanging in her bedroom. It reads (in part):

> I have the courage to . . .
> Embrace my strengths
> Get excited about life
> Enjoy giving and receiving love
> Face and transform my fears
> Ask for help and support when I need it
> Spring free of the Superwoman Trap
> Trust myself
> Make my own decisions and choices
> Befriend myself
> Realize that I have emotional and practical
>   rights
> Talk as nicely to myself as I do to my plants
> Communicate lovingly with understanding as
>   my goal
> Honor my own needs. . . .
> Treat myself with respect and teach others
>   to do the same

Fill my own cup first, then nourish
    others from the overflow
Own my own excellence
Plan for the future but live in the present
Value my intuition and wisdom
Know that I am lovable
Develop healthy, supportive relationships
Make forgiveness a priority
Accept myself as I am now.[2]

Now, that's a poem! An offering of *everything* we could possibly do to live more gently with ourselves. If we could do all that Sue recommends here, we would be so enlightened, so divine, we'd be floating like angels in the biosphere, rather than walking upon the earth. The reality is we usually do the opposite of what she suggests, and we do so over and over again. For, in reality, we are earthly women who struggle, stumble, and fall short of the high ideals we create for ourselves. Sue knows this better than anyone perhaps, because, daily, she invites herself to live more gently, to accept herself as she is, a glorious work in progress, a holy woman "with plans to expand." She does so with exemplary self-compassion and extends a big-sisterly hand to help us do the same.

Compassion is the key and our ticket to wholeness. Compassion is not a word I grew up with or thought much about until my forays into Buddhist teachings years ago. Though the concept came up again and again, I gave it no heed. I took it to mean something we must show toward others. In fact, any dictionary would define it as such: "The deep feeling of sharing the suffering of another; to have mercy for someone."[3] I understood how important it was for any of us to show compassion to others. What I missed altogether was how important it is to feel and offer compassion to ourselves.

I interpret Sue's maxim "Live gently" to mean just this—we must be compassionate toward ourselves. To demonstrate unconditional mercy when we make a choice that leads us away from our truest self. To be consistently kind, loving, and patient—to ourselves. Or, as Joan Borysenko, another mentor featured in this book, would vow, "I will remember to be gentle with myself with all the tenderness, respect, and love that I would give my only child."[4]

Sue describes this compassionate stance as "befriending" ourselves. "I believe it is essential," she says, "that you become a loving and tolerant friend to yourself. Do *you* act as a sheltering tree in your own life? Take a moment to think about how you treat your friends. Do you express the same kindness and consideration toward yourself? Many of us hold a deep-rooted belief that we don't deserve to be loved. 'They' deserve friendship, but for some unfathomable reason, we don't. This is a false belief. We are worthy of love. We *do* deserve our own support and friendship."[5]

Befriending requires an *attitude* of lovingkindness toward one's self, as Sue points out, personified by *acts* of lovingkindness. If we're honest, we'd likely admit that we have often been unkind to ourselves. We've pushed ourselves beyond healthy limits to be the perfect wife, mother, daughter, sister, friend, neighbor, employee, volunteer, community leader, and more; all roles we think we should play in life to be a "good person," to be liked and accepted by others, especially by our family, peers, and coworkers. To be perceived as successful, to be of service to others, and to make a difference in the world. Sue and I have both experienced this drive.

By following her lead, we can strip out the unkind attitudes and expectations we hold for ourselves. Pushing ourselves to exhaustion, caring for everyone but ourselves, and setting impossibly high standards for ourselves is not healthy. According to author Sarah Ban Breathnach, it is self-destructive. "Perfectionism is self-abuse of the highest order," she states in *Simple Abundance* (another wonderful guide to living more gently). These are hard words to hear. None of us wants to admit that we could really be so mean to ourselves. It is up to each of us to put an end to our own self-abuse—to be tender and loving to ourselves so that our truest self, a peaceful and loving self, can emerge.

As the title of Sue's poem "The Courage to Be Myself" indicates, living gently may not be an easy task. It is true, though, that living gently, living compassionately with ourselves, takes great courage. Why? Because most of us live in societies that do not advocate gentle living. We are not taught how to live gently, nor is doing so valued. Instead, we find ourselves, even from childhood, focused on achievement, on accomplishments, on doing, being, and having more. Excessive busyness characterizes our days, and the pace of our lives increases year by year. Faster and faster we go; busier and busier we get.

Living gently, on the other hand, asks us to let go of inner and external pressures to do and be more. It invites us to let go of anything that causes stress and overwhelms us. Anything that keeps us sourced in the ego and its companions of frustration and anger. Anything that keeps us disconnected from our spirit and its core qualities of inner peace, love, and joy. Living gently advocates slowing down so that we can live in a way that honors our innermost desires and our innate rhythm. Doing so enables us to live in the moment and savor each day as a precious gift from the Spirit; to stop and smell the roses before it's too late.

The truth of the matter is most of us don't arrive at this place easily. In fact, most of us don't arrive of our own free will at all. "We go kicking and screaming into gentleness," Sue reminds me on the phone. We are having a conversation about how she finally got off the roller coaster of life and started being kinder to herself. Not surprisingly, she tells me that it was through personal crisis that she was led to "live gently." She describes this time as the worst time in her life, "The hugest dark night of the soul. I had just found out that my husband was having an affair with my best friend. Ha! Some best friend! In actuality, it was the beginning of an entirely new life. I just didn't know it at the time.

"I remember sitting on the floor in front of the sliding glass door in my home, wrapped in a blanket, my forehead pressed to the cool glass. I was singing softly to myself, chanting, crying, certain my life was over. I kept asking why, crying out for divine relief from the pain, and I received a profound answer: 'I love you,' a voice said. 'Why can't *you* love *you*?'" The "I" was God, who, ever-so-gently, reminded her that even though she had been humanly betrayed, she was divinely loved and worthy of that love. Most importantly, she was deserving of her own love.

From that moment on, Sue tells me, she shifted course. She began to gentle her life and do the things for herself she had never done before. "Living gently," Sue tells me, "is really about loving yourself. And I needed to do that." She began to honor herself, noticing what activities made her feel good and loving toward herself, incorporating things that nourished her and her spirit. "It was the first time I realized I was actually more introverted than extroverted, and that it was okay. So I spent more time alone than ever before, read things I never read before. I prayed, meditated, and slowed down almost to a crawl. I wrote extensively in my journals or on napkins or whatever else was available." Sue got in touch with gentle practices that nurtured her whole self—body, mind, and soul—and when she did, everything in her life began to change.

"I gave myself permission to be more contemplative. Actually, 'introspective' might be a better word. To be quieter, and to seek solitude when I needed it. The introspection showed me I needed to fold up my pink tutu and climb out of the oldest-child, buoy-the-family-up center ring and find out who I really was." In time, this slowing down and gentling enabled her to get in touch with her highest purpose. She began her spiritual quest, went to graduate school, and eventually became a psychotherapist.

It is true that personal crises often bring us to the crossroads where new travel plans—permissions—must be granted if we are going to truly live as our sacred selves. Life comes to a screeching halt and we are forced by circumstance to take an honest look at ourselves and how we are living. But any wake-up call can only work its divine magic upon us if we allow it to. We must surrender to its force, as Sue attests, and trust—trust that we're being given an opportunity to rediscover our glorious self, trust that we'll be delivered by this very crisis, as she was, from the ravages of "too much." In fact, I guarantee that every woman featured in this book has done the same. Perhaps you have, as well. But did we learn anything from it? Did we take this opportunity to slow down and create space in our lives, within ourselves, to see and feel more clearly? Or did we climb back on the roller coaster and go around again because we thought we had no other choice? It is crucial at this passage of our journey that we give ourselves permission to slow down and be alone. To take time apart from others to get clear about what has happened and who it is we are being invited to become. To restore ourselves and return to a personal sense of equilibrium.

Anne Morrow Lindbergh (author and wife of aviator Charles Lindbergh) is another woman who grants us permission to be gentle with ourselves. Every year Anne spent two weeks by herself on retreat on an island off the Florida coast. Alone, she walked the beaches, gathered shells, and mulled over her life. With nature as her teacher, she journaled about what it means to be a woman. Her book *Gift from the Sea* is a series of essays about what she discovered on retreat.

One of her reflections on a moon shell she'd found on a beach walk offers wisdom about the importance of solitude to restore and reclaim ourselves. Anne wrote:

> Moon Shell. . . . You will make me think,
> with your smooth circles winding inward
> to the tiny core, of the island I lived on for a
> few weeks. You will say to me "Solitude."
> You will remind me that I must try to be
> alone for part of each year—even a week
> or a few days, and for a part of each day,
> even for an hour or a few minutes, in order

to keep my core, my center, my island
quality.

Anne's powerful words speak to the universal feminine need for sacred space and time spent blessedly
alone. "You remind me," she went on to say,

> that unless I keep the island quality intact
> somewhere within me, I will have little to
> give my husband, my children, my friends
> or the world at large. You will remind me
> that woman must be still, as the axis of a
> wheel in the midst of her activities; that
> she must be the pioneer in achieving this
> stillness, not only for her own salvation,
> but for the salvation of family life, of
> society, perhaps even of our civilization.[6]

"Island quality" is what Anne called it—this sense
of being self-contained in a good, solid way. We find it
most easily when we are apart from others. We become
beautiful islands unto ourselves, as she did, when we no
longer depend upon others for our emotional well-being
or for affirmation. When we are self-sustaining and
can give ourselves what we need to be nourished and
honored, our island quality grows. Anne's lovely prose
inspired me to give myself more "island time." I did so
by creating daily "mini-retreats"—an hour or two spent
alone with myself at the beginning or end of each day. I
also gave myself permission to take occasional weekend
retreats. "Island times" such as these can provide the
sacred time and space needed to begin to gentle ourselves, gentle our lives.

Wayne Muller refers to special times such as these as
"Sabbaths." Sabbath is something we have forgotten, a

soulful practice of rest and restoration we've left behind
in the name of progress. Granted, most religions have
a sacred time set aside to connect with self and Spirit
(a holy day, feast day, or worship day). This is not the
only Sabbath of which Muller writes in his book titled
Sabbath: "Sabbath is time consecrated with our attention,
our mindfulness, honoring those quiet forces of grace or
spirit that sustain and heal us." He also points out that
it is through Sabbath that we are able to remember how
we are most deeply nourished. "We are able to see more
clearly the shape and texture of the people and things
before us."[7]

Sabbath time is vital to our well-being and our
connection to Spirit. Due to the structure and pace of
our lives, in truth, we have lost the art of creating such
opportunities for ourselves. Yet, there are a myriad of
ways to create Sabbath moments if we want to experience their benefits and joys. Sue suggests we might start
by leaving "white spaces" for ourselves.

> When we open our daily calendars, how
> much white space [unscheduled time] do
> we see? Without white space in which to
> relax and be, we become overstimulated
> and sometimes even addicted to intensity—
> like a shark constantly moving even in
> sleep. . . . In order to grow emotionally and
> spiritually, we must make white space a
> priority. It is in the privacy of white space
> that our hearts heal and expand. In the
> quiet of white space we can hear the urg-
> ings of our higher selves and receive the
> mysterious teachings from the feminine
> within.[8]

The world will not slow down long enough to hand us such sacred moments. We alone must shape our days (or some portion of them) so that we can be nourished, rested, restored. Taking back the hours of our days and re-centering them in the Spirit is one of the ways we can begin to live more gently with ourselves. Truly, we can make our days and nights any way we want them. Sue's book *The Woman's Book of Soul* offers us many ideas for creating Sabbath moments. It all comes down to a matter of choice. Even if we share our homes with busy others or have hectic schedules, if we desire inner peace and spiritual connection badly enough, sacred moments can be found. It is up to us to seek them out. It is up to us to love ourselves enough to give us what we need to feel whole.

Perhaps, though, the most powerful method for living more gently with ourselves is through becoming more "mindful." Mindfulness is the ability to live in the present moment, where we are intimately connected with our most peaceful, loving self, nary a worry or "should" in sight. It is both a mindset and a learned set of practices. Much to my delight, as I was gathering the information for this chapter, I discovered Sue was in the throes of writing a new book— should I be surprised?— on mindfulness. I shared this with her, and she was as pleased as I that holy synchronicity had happened once again. "I love being part of 'Wonderful Weirdness!'" she laughs.

I can't help but wonder, what brings her to explore mindfulness right now at this juncture of her life? "I was asked to write a book on it, and I leaped at the chance, because I know that what we most have to learn, we often get to teach."

Sue readily admits that mindfulness has not been an easy thing for her, but it has been transformative. When she sent me the unedited early chapters of *The Mindful Woman* to take a peek at, I had a big chuckle as I read her account of struggling to write the introduction to her book. Though she had intended to sit down and have a very present-centered morning writing about mindfulness, she was still trying to do too many things at once. "I caught myself stumbling over my credit card number while giving it to a catalog saleswoman because I was simultaneously bringing up my e-mails, scrubbing allergic cat-boogers off my computer screen, and obsessing how I was going to start the introduction.

"That was an amusing and harmless little episode," she adds, "but others are not so funny. When I'm too exhausted to sleep because I'm overcommitted, obsessively worried, resentful, or trying to solve the woes of the world—or, more likely, those of my immediate family—that's not funny."[9]

But because, Sue admits, she is gradually becoming more mindful, she was able to catch herself in that crazed moment. She noticed how she was becoming *absent*minded in that moment, instead of mind*ful*. She took her own advice and engaged in a powerful four-step process to come back to the present moment: *stop—look—listen—feel*. Sue explains that with this method, we can awaken ourselves and stop living on autopilot. "We absolutely must shift our attitude and focus so that we are not sleep-living any longer."

We begin the process of becoming more mindful by noticing, being very aware of where we are in the moment; by paying attention, detail by detail, to what's going on around us. We observe our thoughts and feelings, too, especially if they are scattered or frenzied. To calm and focus ourselves, we connect with our breath, which will bring us back into body awareness. Given a few moments, we can relax into the present and see the world in front of us with new eyes.

Present-centered awareness through mindfulness allows us to slow down enough to experience the sacred all around us. Sue believes there are as many ways to nurture mindfulness as there are women in the world, and we must each find our own way. The point is to begin. We can *stop—look—listen—feel* anywhere, she advises, "while doing anything—ironing, working at the computer, making love, cleaning the litter box, in class, dancing, cooking, driving. . . ."[10]

Mindfulness enables us to be more present to ourselves and our world—to be fully aware of what we are thinking, feeling, and doing—all for the purpose of living more gently with ourselves and others. By being mindful, we "pay attention on purpose" so that we don't miss one precious moment of our lives, to enable us to feel the pure joy of being alive and, at the same time, fully present to the difficult moments so we can find truth in them.

As I read the pages of her manuscript, I found myself reflecting back on all I have learned from Sue over the years. I was reminded of where our journey together began—with my inability to be kind to myself—and how different my life is today. She, more than anyone else, has taught me how to *befriend* myself, to *honor* myself, and to give myself *permission* to make new choices. It is Sue's voice I often hear in my own head when the threat of busyness or overwhelm comes to call. "Are you talking nicely to yourself?" she'll ask. "Is this a kind choice?" Her words, especially those expressed in her beautifully penned poem, never fail to bring me back to my truest self.

"I have the courage to be myself. . . . To feel all of my feelings and act on them appropriately. . . . Choose what is right for me. . . . Grow through my challenges. . . . Treat myself with respect. . . . Accept myself as I am now. . . ." Sue Patton Thoele invites us to lovingly embrace ourselves as we are, clothing ourselves with the fifth Transformational Truth:

I Cultivate Compassion for Myself

Gentleness toward oneself does result in self-compassion. Sue can attest to that. And, now, thankfully, so can I. Living gently offers a side benefit, as well. It enables us to take ourselves and our lives more lightly. This is one of the things I admire and enjoy about Sue, and something, I admit, I still need to grow into. She is lighthearted, childlike, and joy-filled. Even when life gets tough, she doesn't allow herself to wallow in pity for too long, to feel "beige," as she calls it, on any given day. It seems that her ability to treat herself gently has brought more fun into her life, along with helping her maintain a terrific sense of humor.

Sue shared with me once that every year she treats herself to a dolphin swim and that she has done so for eleven years. I often think how perfectly suited this is to her—frolicing with the creatures who epitomize the gentleness of spirit and lightness of being she herself represents. One evening, not too long ago, I headed down to the coastline in front of my house to savor the sunset, an important ritual that brings gentle closure to my day, and my thoughts turned to Sue. I wondered if she might be in Bimini at this very moment, at the water's edge like myself, preparing for her annual dolphin swim. I squinted into the sun's descending rays and imagined what that amazing experience might be like for her . . .

I imagine her out in the Atlantic Ocean, floating in that blue-green abyss, a huge, childlike grin upon her face as she swims happily with her dolphin companions. I imagine her accepting their loving looks in return with glee. And then, much to my surprise, I see her nimbly climb on the back of one, looking very much like the curly-haired Miss Frizzle of *Magic School Bus* fame, complete with polka-dot bathing suit and flippers. Pulling a yellow pair of goggles down over her eyes, she turns to look at me, blows a kiss, and offers a joyous wave. A delicate kick from her finned heels and they're off, riding the waves, heading into the sunset together—gentleness and joy embodied in a well-matched pair.

Reflection Questions

1. Are you gentle with yourself? In what ways? In what ways are you unkind to yourself?
2. What is your current ability to attend to your needs? To honor your true desires? What prevents you from doing so?
3. If you could create a personal Sabbath day for yourself, what would that day look like? Feel like?

Peaceful Pause

Being Enough

Stand in front of a mirror and allow yourself to relax into the image of the woman who looks back at you. Take a few nurturing breaths in and out as you settle more deeply into your body. Be comfortable and at ease with yourself. As you continue to breathe slowly and evenly, allow your attention to linger on your face in the mirror. Look into your eyes with tenderness, with compassion. Trust that the Divine One is supporting you in this pure acceptance of yourself as you are now.

Silently repeat to yourself:

> Because I am a woman growing into my fullness, growing into my truest self, I will treat myself like the gentlest of flowers.

> Today, I release any shoulds that plague me, which tell me I must *do* to gain approval from others or to feel good about myself.

> Today, I give myself permission to fully and completely *be*. To be as I am now. To be myself.

> In this very moment, *I am enough.*

truth
six

I Experience the Divine in Everything and Everyone

Daphne Rose Kingma

*The day of my spiritual awakening was the day I
saw all things in God and God in all things.*

Mechtild of Magdeburg

I met Daphne Rose Kingma, "The Love Doctor," when my own loving relationship was in peril. Our coming together was a marvelous synchronicity, she an internationally renowned expert on all matters of the heart, and me a disenchanted lover. I had read many of her books, ever hopeful that real love, love based upon spiritual principles, might someday be mine. Daphne, as luck would have it, was a good friend of my (former) mother-in-law. Ironically, the correspondence and conversations we shared over the years never got around to the subject of my own intimate relationship.

In 1998, as I was I putting the final touches on my book on self-nurturing for women, I made contact with her. I was interested in talking with her further about the importance of self-love, especially for women recovering from emotional dependency. After a few letters back and forth—it was hard to track her down, world-traveler that she is—I was finally able to arrange a face-to-face meeting in her hometown of Santa Barbara, California. I recall my excitement at meeting the famous Daphne, author of nearly a dozen books on love, radio show host, frequent guest expert on television talk shows, and therapist to the stars. She was the closest thing our family had to a celebrity, and I couldn't wait to meet her.

On a balmy February evening in 1999, my sister Linda and I waited for her to arrive at the little French bistro we'd agreed upon. When she arrived, she did not disappoint: Gliding in, she was tall, blonde, and stunningly beautiful. "Dressed to the nines," as they say. All heads in the room turned at the sight of this exquisite woman, whose warm smile and kind response touched everyone who acknowledged her. It was obvious she was well known, and she accepted the recognition with grace and humility. She recognized me from across the room and waved, seemed to float on air to our table and make herself comfortable, effortlessly drawing us into her loving gaze. Daphne Kingma, unlike anyone I'd ever met, oozed the enchanted love she'd written about in her books. I remember wanting to bask in that emanation of love forever.

For the next hour or so we talked nonstop. We caught up on family news and discussed women's spiritual journeys. Our time together flew by, and before I knew it, the time had come for her to leave. She was embarking the next day on one of her many trips, and she needed to go home to pack. As she gathered up her things, she hesitated a moment, then leaned across the table. She looked deeply at me for a split second, then lowered her gaze and became extremely quiet for what seemed to me like an eternity, though I am sure it was only a few seconds. I didn't know what to say or do, so I simply waited. "I think," she said finally, "we should have a little supper together. Don't you? A light salad?" And with that she hailed the waiter to place our order. Surprised by this change in plans, I was delighted that

Daphne had, for whatever reason, decided to stay so we could chat some more.

I didn't understand at the time what happened within Daphne in those quiet moments to make her change her mind. It seemed as if she had leaned in to discern more deeply whether she should remain or go. It was not until years later that I learned this was precisely what she was doing. She was "feeling" me, an ability she was born with—extreme sensitivity to the essence of another—and she sensed that I wished we could have more time. "I was given the gift of a very highly emotional consciousness and perception," she told me later. "I have conscious memories of myself in infancy; of interactions with others at age one in which I can remember the actual words that were spoken and the emotional energy that was being expressed."

This heightened emotional awareness enabled Daphne to feel everything and everyone in her environment with extremes, including her parents' suffering. I knew she had been raised in Grand Rapids, Michigan, as I had; but I didn't know much more than that about her upbringing. In time, she shared with me that she was the fifth child (and fourth daughter) of a family that was always struggling to make ends meet. While very young, all her siblings had become ill, two with life-threatening diseases. "I was keenly aware of their suffering, their physical, emotional pain," she said. Yet she was also able to see and feel the beauty and pleasure of her parents' intimate relationship, as well as their relationships with each of their children.

Not an easy burden to carry, this highly developed emotional awareness, yet eventually Daphne was able to make sense of her "spiritual gift," as she regards it now.

It was through people, through human relationships, she realized, that she was able to experience the Divine One most profoundly. "The experience of the essence of human beings . . . the majesty, the mystery and complexity of their interactions has always been, for me, the vehicle of my spiritual awareness." She assured me that this can be true for the rest of us as well. Why? Because we are all divinely sourced beings. We are here to experience the Divine One itself in and through one another. Daphne believes that the path of human relationship can be a powerful pathway to self-illumination and to God.

In the summer of 2004, I was finally able to speak with Daphne in depth about this. I eagerly awaited her phone call, but on the morning of our scheduled conversation many things came up to sabotage our time together. Her car had died and was in need of immediate repair; her cell phone kept dropping our calls. We nearly canceled the interview out of sheer frustration, but Daphne persevered—her inner guidance told her to—and we finally connected while she waited for her car to be fixed.

She is seated on a tree stump, in front of the garage on a busy Santa Barbara street, she tells me. I can hear cars zooming by, voices in the background; and I'm not sure how focused she will be to speak with me, considering the setting. But she is—completely. Through the air waves, I can feel her attunement once again, just as I had in the bistro years before. She hones in with intuitive precision to me, my thoughts, even my unspoken feelings, as we talk.

I start by asking her to tell me more about how our human relationships can lead us into a greater experience of the Divine.

She answers my question with a story about her childhood understanding of God. "My experience of spiritual reality then was that my mother was God," she says. "My mother was such a powerful, beautiful, and insistent woman that when I went to Sunday school or heard about God in church, I always thought that that divine and infinitely powerful Being must have been my mother, because she had all those mighty attributes. My earliest sense of the Divine was of a very immediate presence—and a personal one at that."

But eventually the message about the Big God receded into the background. Through the experiences she had observing the people sitting in church, Daphne was drawn into the humanity around her—not surprising for a young girl who could "feel" the essence of others. "Suddenly everything was about human relationships," she tells me. "Even hearing the stories about Jesus, I was thinking, well, okay, what's really going on here is that Jesus is having these very extraordinary relationships with people. They are sharing powerful, miraculous experiences. They are seeing one another's sacredness."

Eventually Daphne realized that her connection to the world of Spirit was being mediated through experience, through other human beings—the "strangers" from church who had no children but gave her, when she was six, a tiny locket shaped in the form of a book, a prophecy of her writing life to come; the woman who took her to see her friend as she lay dying and how the dying woman blessed her; the boy in school who taught her how to paint. Her life's purpose, as she explains it today, is an expression of this early understanding. "We engage in the world of the numinous through our experiences of one another," she says. "If we pay attention, we see how the world of Spirit is continuously embodied in our human interactions."

The crux of Daphne's message is this: "Each of us comes home to our most sacred self through being in relationship—through loving one another. Not by isolating ourselves, going up to the mountaintop and studying alone for years in a cave with our legs crossed, but by being in the everyday world where human experience constantly asks us to learn how to love one another, to be gracious and thoughtful and kind, to be generous and humorous and wise, to listen, to share, to embrace. This is where Love, Spirit, God operates." In fact, her life's purpose as she explains it today is an expression of this understanding. "I believe I'm here," she reveals, "to teach people how to love, to teach the gestures and skills and attitudes and actions that allow us to experience Love as it keeps expressing itself through all our relationship connections."

We begin this journey into love, Daphne explains, by first learning to love ourselves. "It is the difficulties of our childhoods," she says, "that cause us to need to do this." Indeed, it was her own struggle with self-love, eloquently written about in her book *Loving Yourself*, that became the template for her teaching to others.

Learning to love yourself is a process, she says. It takes time. "In my own life, for example, I always felt I was superfluous and, in fact, a burden to my family. It wasn't because my parents didn't love me. Indeed, they both showed me many beautiful expressions of love. Rather, it was because the circumstances of our life were very difficult." When she was little, all four of her siblings were extremely ill. Her mother served tirelessly as a nursemaid to each of her sick children, while Daphne sat upon the stairs day after day, patiently waiting for the time when her mother could come and feed her. "I felt so sorry for my mother that after taking care of everyone and everything else, there was still another person— me—who needed her attention and care. I began to wonder if it wouldn't be easier for everyone if I hadn't been born, or if I'd just disappear." She responded to her parents' circumstances by trying to take up as little of their time, energy, space, and money as she could. "I practiced the art of being invisible. Trying to disappear is a long way from loving yourself."[1]

Daphne encourages us to learn the necessary skills of caring for ourselves, both physically and emotionally. It is also important for us to understand our personalities on a psychological/emotional level so we can heal the wounds of our childhood, establish healthy, new beliefs about our self and worth, and learn how we desire and deserve to live. This "work of self-love" is a tireless work, and it may take an entire lifetime to engage it, to undo the workings of the ego and our wounded personalities, but this is the one thing we are all called to do. According to Daphne, this is just one level of loving yourself. There is another higher, more spiritual level of self-love. It is a level of loving to which we as holy women aspire because it is the only form of self-love that will bring us into greater wholeness. "Loving yourself in this way," she says, "is a matter of loving your *essence*."

What does that mean, to love our essence? It means to raise ourselves up beyond the dramas of everyday life, beyond the petty human interactions we have with others, so we can view ourselves and one another as the divine beings we are. "This essence is beyond all the psychological dramas we've endured. It is beyond all our heartaches and woes, beyond our achievements, even beyond the legacies we'll leave behind. This essence is nameless, faceless, radiant, and eternal," says Daphne. This you is Spirit embodied in human form. This you is *Love.*

But what, you might ask, if you don't feel like Love? (Much less lovely, lovable, loved, or loving?) What if you are not in touch with your essence? Where in the world do you begin? You begin exactly where you are by noticing the person who is standing right in front of you, because in their eyes, if you look very closely, you will see yourself. All aspects of yourself are reflected there, your wounded, fearful, insecure, ego self—as well as your glorious, confident, peaceful, loving, spiritual self—your essence. Through being in relationship with others, you will get to see yourself in all your human limitations, as well as in all your divine potentiality. Every other person can see themselves in you in this way, too. For as spirit/human beings, we are perfect mirrors for one another. Let me explain how I learned this firsthand with Daphne's assistance.

Do you recall the description of my first meeting with her at the bistro in Santa Barbara—how she floated across the room, turning heads as she went? Witnessing her do that, just being herself in her unique expression, I got to see me in mine. But mine wasn't as stunning as hers. In fact, my uniqueness in that moment was pretty stained, tainted with shades of insecurity, inferiority, even jealousy. Daphne being Daphne pushed all my buttons, so to speak, and brought up all my adolescent self-conscious feelings about not being tall, blonde, and lovely like she was. I was short, dark, and round, and I'd always struggled with that. Not to mention that she was exquisitely dressed, California style. Watching her come toward me in all her glory brought up feelings in me of being nothing more than a frumpily dressed Midwestern waif. Surely, I was a weed compared to her rose! As a result, I found myself shrinking down into myself, not unlike what Daphne used to do on the stairs, waiting for her beautiful God/mother to pay attention to her. In fact, this is probably why I have very little memory of our conversation that evening. I was so darn self-conscious I could hardly pay attention to what was being said!

Recalling this encounter years later was a defining moment for me. Thankfully, I was able to see that my response to Daphne had been nothing more than my ego's response. Just one more effort on behalf of my false self to keep me feeling small, insignificant, lost in the shadow of a glorious other.

But because Daphne was Daphne, she served as my mirror. With her standing right in front of me, a crystal-clear version of her truest self—confident and radiant—I was able to see myself in her reflection. This is what happens when any of us enters into relationship with another. Just by being ourselves, we give the other person a chance to see which version of themselves they are experiencing in that moment.

In meeting Daphne, I was given a powerful opportunity to see myself clearly. And I was given a choice. I could ignore what I saw in the mirror about my own self—vast insecurity—and continue to operate as that wounded self. Or, I could accept the invitation to heal and relinquish that particular ego trait, one that had kept me imprisoned for years. I could choose to love myself more, to love myself as essence—or not.

The choice of how to respond to this opportunity is always ours. I chose to accept Daphne's (unconscious) invitation that day to begin the journey of loving myself more. Only through learning to love myself a little bit more with each passing year was I able to feel confident enough to take Daphne off the pedestal I'd placed her on and place us side by side, joined as one spirit-being, essence to essence. Any of us can do the same.

In *The Future of Love*, Daphne explains that we are at a pivotal moment in our planetary history. "We are being asked to mature into our true wholeness, as human beings who are in fact divine eternal souls, and we are being invited to do this in *relationship*." Any interaction we have with anyone, carefully examined, will reveal how well we are embodying either our sacred self or our ego self in that moment. "A journey we started as personalities," she writes, "we are now being asked to finish as souls."[2]

By noticing the feelings that come up when we are with another person, we are given a unique opportunity to take a closer look at ourselves. Until now, our tendency may have been to focus on what *they* are doing wrong, what *they* are doing to make us feel bad about ourselves. The invitation that is being offered at this juncture of our journey as holy women is to stop pointing the finger at someone else for making us feel less-than-wonderful and look in the mirror of our own self-perceptions. In my case, Daphne did nothing to make me feel bad about myself. In fact, quite the opposite. By being her truest self—a self that is naturally beautiful, warm, confident, and caring—I felt her love and honest regard. Through her very *essence*, she invited me to step into my own.

This is what we can all do for one another—we can
serve as mirrors. Through the mirror of our everyday
interactions, we reflect back how well each of us is
embodying our truest self—or not. When I am with you,
if my thoughts and feelings have run amok with anger,
insecurity, suspicion, resentment, or judgment (qualities
of the ego), I am not connected to my truest self. And
the same will be true for you when you interact with
me. On the other hand, if our thoughts and feelings are
ripe with inner peace, appreciation, forgiveness, trust,
or openheartedness (qualities of the Spirit, of God), you
and I will be experiencing ourselves and each other
as that. As Sri Nisargadatta Maharaj once said, "You
are love itself—when you are not afraid." This is what
Daphne reminds us of, too. "We are love, and everything
we suffer and endure, go through or dream of is here to
remind us of that single final fact."[3]

We are love. You are, and I am, too. Each of us is a
pure spark of divine love just waiting to be fanned from
ember to flame. This is what we do for one another—
especially through the vehicle of our intimate relationship. We fan each other into a full-blown fiery expression
of the God who dwells within us. Each of us in our own
way is trying to connect with our spirit, with God as we
understand it, ever more deeply. The truth of the matter
is, if we are unable to see each person who comes into
our lives as an expression of the Sacred One, perhaps
it is because we still have not embraced ourselves as
sacred. We may not have arrived at the shores of our
own self-love. For how can we possibly experience a
profound love of others if we cannot feel similarly about
ourselves? If we can honestly admit that we are not yet

able to view others as sacred, then we may have more inner journeying to do.

This is the truth that Daphne conveys each time I have been in her presence or through her letters. I feel her envisioning me, experiencing me, holding *me* as sacred, and then by her very example, inviting me to do the same with others. And when we are able to truly perceive the Divine in everyone, our world begins to take a dramatic turn. It morphs from ordinary to extraordinary; it becomes a magical place teeming with second-by-second miracles, because we perceive every human encounter as a holy encounter. Each interaction with another becomes an expression of the Divine, a potential joining of spirits for one another's greater growth. "Our relationships show how the life of the Spirit is always operative in our midst," she tells me.

Carl Jung explained it this way: "The meeting of two personalities is like the contact of two chemical substances; if there is any reaction, both are transformed." When Daphne and I met, when any two of us meet and come together, we are transformed. Through the synchronicity of our meeting, we enter into a divinely sourced relationship, which, if attended to, will take us more deeply into our truest selves. The key to understanding why we have come together is to be receptive—to remain open to what we can learn from one another.

"In fact, it is all about being receptive," Daphne says. "And receptivity, of course, is a very feminine quality because it is the essence of the feminine to be open, to be able to be filled and transformed by what presents itself to you—on a biological level, on a spiritual level, and on an emotional level. The feminine is the capacity for complete and total surrender," and that, she explains, is why "no matter what your biological gender—male or female—whenever you come into the Presence of the Divine, you are being invited to occupy the stance of the feminine consciousness, which is about willingness to surrender in order to be transformed. And when we surrender to what appears right in front of us as a person or a situation, there is always an opportunity to engage ourselves as spirit *with* Spirit."

The process of re-imaging ourselves, each other, and the world as pure divine expression takes time. As Sr. Joan Chittister has said, "It takes a lifetime to understand that God is what is standing in front of me." Understanding that God is, indeed, a version of you and of me in *form*, in a human body, is something that often escapes us. "Rather than seeing the beauty of the gift," Daphne says, "the generosity of the teaching, the miracle of the soul who is crossing our path, we often see only the person who is holding us up at the check-out counter, disappointing us in our marriage, refusing to feed our ego, or unable to empathize with us." God, the Divine Spirit, is everywhere in the world around us, in all the human situations in which we find ourselves. Receptivity and openness are the holy woman traits we need to cultivate in order to be able to receive the divine teachings that reside in each of them.

"I evaluate my spiritual life," Daphne continues from her tree stump outside the garage, "by the amount of miracles that are occurring in my actual physical life. What I mean by miracles is powerful synchronicities. My relationship with you, Jan, is certainly one of those. No doubt about it. Especially when you consider we were brought together by your former mother-in-law, and we didn't meet until more than thirty years later.

"Our meeting today is also a miracle. I really tried to be available today, to stay open despite the challenging circumstances, because despite all our difficulties connecting—the car, the phone—I really wanted to speak with you again. It seemed impossible, because I also needed to flow with the needs of the day and get my car fixed. But here I am, sitting outside in front of the mechanic's shop having this transcendent experience of talking with you.

"I live in a world of miracles. We all do. It's just a matter of remaining open to them."

In every situation, in every human encounter, we can experience the sacred. There is always holiness when we come together as human beings. According to Daphne, there can even be holiness when our relationships fall apart. In fact, she shares with me that it was through her decision to divorce her husband many years ago, that she was taken to the precipice of new growth and spiritual understanding. "I remember thinking at the time: 'Now I'm doing the one thing I never imagined doing, the one thing I'm not sure I can ever forgive myself for doing. I'm breaking the only promise I thought I'd keep all my life.' And yet," she says, "there was this voice, this inner knowing that said, 'Daphne, step over the abyss. Everything will be fine on the other side.'" And so she did, moving, as she tells me, "through passages when everything felt so dark that all I could do was proceed on faith. Clearly, the life I'd been living needed to die, and clearly the life I would come to live was still invisible. But had I not been open, receptive to the voice of my intuition, I never would have moved on to the joyful life of serving and loving that has followed.

"It's *all* about being receptive," she concludes, "about surrendering to what you can't see yet."

As my own journey into self-love evolved over the years, with Daphne's assistance, I found myself better able to love others in more expansive ways than I had in the past, to see them as spiritual beings with their own sacred journeys to be lived. Yet, as is often the case when any of us shift and change, growing into a brighter version of ourselves, our relationships will inevitably shift and change as well; and my growth, too, meant letting go of a marriage. And when that time came, Daphne's wisdom in *Coming Apart* guided me through a three-year process of learning to let go with love, and her *Future of Love* enabled me to take a giant leap of faith into the arms of a new relationship, the most profound, unconditionally loving relationship I have ever known—with my beloved husband, Brad.

It is a relationship sourced in the spiritual principles I have always longed to live in the context of a real relationship, and, in 2006, Brad and I were able to pen our own book on the subject, *Perfect Love*, which provides couples with guidance to create their own enlightened model of relationship—a true spiritual partnership. I attribute much of what I have learned about the power of relationship to heal and transform to Daphne. Blessedly, my relationship with her over the years has allowed me to know, finally, what Victor Hugo wrote many years ago: "To love another is to touch the face of God."

A miraculous universe is Daphne's reality, and she assures me it can be the same for any of us. We need only open our eyes, hearts, and arms a bit wider to welcome it in. We live in a universe full of divine encounters with ordinary people through ordinary events, all disguised as the sacred. Some will be joyful, others will be painful, as her own journey attests. "Some of the journey will be arduous," she wisely tells me. "But there will always be angels along the way."

Through her writings and her life, Daphne Rose Kingma invites us to expand our awareness and embrace the sixth Transformational Truth:

I Experience the Divine in Everything and Everyone

As we spoke that day in 2004, Daphne sitting on her stump on a busy street in Santa Barbara, I in my quiet office in Michigan, I was invited into her magical universe to witness a shower of sacred moments. We had been speaking of the power of synchronistic meetings and connections between people, when suddenly, there was a break in our conversation, and I heard her moving about, speaking to someone else.

"Thank you, Ricardo, that's so kind of you," she says. Then, turning her attention back to me, she explains what has just happened. "See," she laughs, "there's a little miracle right now, a living example of what I've just been talking about. I'm sitting out here on a tree stump, and a lovely man just came out of his place of business and brought me a beautiful little stool to sit on."

I hear her voice break with emotion as she continues, "And this action brings tears to my heart, because it is nothing less than love, pure love, and it's the hundreds of examples like this throughout my life that have communicated to me the unequivocal presence of the Divine."

Whenever I think of Daphne now, this is the tender image that comes to mind: her long, lanky form folded in upon itself to fit atop a tree stump under a shade tree, her heart wide open to the Universe, alert to its holy offerings. In a grace-filled moment she is given the gift of a stool from a total stranger so she can be more comfortable. "Do you see that?" she remarked. "An angel. . . . Moment by moment, we can all be angels to one another."

That we are, I think to myself. Divinity embodied. Daphne has, most certainly, been that to me, to all of us. An angel, an emissary of true Love.

Reflection Questions

1. Where are you in the process of learning to love yourself?
2. Have you experienced moments when someone served as a mirror for you to look more clearly at yourself? What was that like? How did that revelation impact you?
3. How well are you able to see the divinity of another person?

Peaceful Pause

Seeing Others as Sacred

Imagine for a moment that you have put on a pair of special eyeglasses that enable you to see each person who crosses your path in a new way. The glasses are comfortable and light to wear. They have the effect of revealing the person in front of you with soft eyes. When you look through these lenses, you see the unique way that Spirit has come into the world in the form of this particular human being. Let your eyes roam over them. Take time to marvel at the ingenuity required to make each person such a special rendition of Spirit.

Offer the following silent prayer:

> May I see the divine spark within each person who comes into my life. May I offer them unconditional love and acceptance as my Higher Power does for me.

truth
seven

I Know Divine Assistance Is Available to Me at All Times

Doreen Virtue

We shall find peace. We shall hear angels.
We shall see the sky sparkling with diamonds.

Anton Chekhov

I was struggling to begin. How was I to write this chapter featuring the "Angel Lady," Doreen Virtue? There was so much I wanted to say about her, about the higher realms, about what connecting to divine guidance can mean for us as holy women.

There was also much I was hesitant to say. Though it has been reported in polls that 95 percent of Americans believe in angels, the subject of actual angelic encounters seems to stir up controversy. Over the years, as I had mentioned angels to various people, their usual response was eye rolling or an all-knowing smirk with a silent, "Oh, she's one of *those* . . ." behind it. Or, it was a piece of advice, like the one I received from a clerk in my local Christian bookstore: "You do *not* want to go *there*," she warned. Heaven knows, I did not want to go *there*, wherever *there* was, nor did I want to risk anyone's ire. Just as I was beginning to wallow in pools of self-doubt—not about the existence of angels, but what to say about them here without alienating readers—the telephone rang.

It was Richard Williams calling from *Angels on Earth* magazine. He asked me if I was ready to arrange my interview with its editor-in-chief, Colleen Hughes. I had called a few weeks earlier to speak with her about the publication and all their loyal readers who, I later learned, submitted more than a thousand articles a month on personal encounters with angels.

Hearing Richard's voice, I chuckle at the synchronicity of his call. Here I am smack-dab in the middle of self-doubt, and the angels show up. "Yes," Richard confirms when I tell him what's going on with me. "The angels are all around us to help, aren't they?" he laughs. His warm and centered presence bolsters my flagging confidence. Yet I am ultimately able to write these words upon the page because of Doreen Virtue and her courageous journey to live her truths—many of them issued from the lips of the angels themselves.

I was first exposed to Doreen when she presented at a women's conference in Warren, Michigan, in 1996. She was speaking about her book *Constant Craving*, an insightful look at our emotional relationship with food. I found her message fascinating and took it to heart, looking at my own "cravings" and what they might reveal about my physical and emotional well-being. When I saw Doreen, she was svelte and physically quite beautiful by anyone's standards. She had struggled with her weight most of her life and had finally broken through that imposing barrier to restore her self-esteem. Little did I know when I saw her that day how she had just emerged victorious from another lifelong struggle— listening to and publicly acknowledging the angels.

I did not learn this until 2004, when I had the opportunity to interview her for a holiday-focused article I was writing on angels. Over the years, I had observed her meteoric rise to fame as a celebrated author and lecturer. I had read a number of her books, having been introduced to the notion of angels by my friend Ellie. Another friend gifted me with a set of Doreen's "Angel Cards." I was excited to speak with her in person because I was curious how she had garnered the courage to publicly represent the angelic realm as she has.

As I speak with her on the telephone, I am delighted to find her warm and sincere, just like I hoped she would be. She is bubbly, energetic, and so passionate about our ability to connect with the angels.

Doreen tells me that she was born clairvoyant, the fourth generation in a line of female metaphysical healers. She was raised with the notion of using prayer and mental thought for healing by both her mother and father, who embraced New Thought principles. Her mother, who was a professional Christian-Science practitioner, spent most of her time healing others. "I was raised with miracles," Doreen says. "As far back as I can remember there was no lid on our spiritual experiences." In fact, she tells me that *she* was the result of a miracle. Her parents had been childless for seven years, and within three weeks of her mother's heartfelt petition for a child at a Church of Religious Science prayer meeting, Doreen was conceived.

I also learn that as a child, angels and guides (deceased loved ones and relatives) spoke to her on a regular basis, but this was not something Doreen dared share with others. When she did, other children laughed at her. "I went into a closet and didn't talk openly about this to anyone, except a few close girlfriends. It was very, very difficult. I wanted to be a healer like my mom, but I didn't dare. I needed to do something socially acceptable [that involved healing], so I became a psychotherapist instead."

Despite her career choice, the angels kept speaking to her. They told Doreen that she was supposed to be teaching about the body-mind-spirit connection and about the angels themselves. "But I'd fight them. 'No, no, no,' I would say. 'You don't understand. People will laugh at me. I'm a successful psychotherapist. I'll lose everything. You angels don't understand what it's like to live on this earth. You don't have bills to pay!'" The last time she argued with them, however, Doreen almost died.

It was July 15, 1995, and she was getting ready to leave her house in Newport Beach, California, to speak at a church in Anaheim. As she did so, one of her angels told her loud and clear to put the top up on her convertible car or it would be stolen. "I was so accustomed to arguing with my angels at that point. Because I was running late for my appointment and the electric motor on my convertible top was broken, I argued with them once again. I told them I didn't have time to put the top up. They argued back; they insisted. I said, 'No, just protect me. Just protect me.'"

What happens next, Doreen tells me, is the pivotal moment of her life, one for which she is now most grateful. "As I was getting out of my car to lock it, I was jumped by two armed men with a gun and a knife. They had a getaway car, and this man accosted me and said that he was going to take my car and my purse." But as Doreen explains, her angels were still there. Even though she had ignored them, they did not abandon her. "They told me to scream with all my might, NOW, and it was such a breakthrough moment, because I finally obeyed my angels and I screamed, louder than I knew I had it in me."

This got the attention of people in the church who came out, scaring the two men away. "So, I just got down on my knees in the parking lot and asked God, 'How can I repay you?'" The reply was the same thing Doreen had heard all of her life: "Teach about the angels." Teach what she knew to be true -that angels are real, here to help us and to guide us whenever we need them. The very next day she was scheduled to speak at a health conference, and she "came out of the closet" as she had promised God and the angels she would. It no longer mattered to her what people would think. "Although I have to admit that I did make a bargain with the angels. 'I will do this for you,' I said, 'but I really want you to protect me. I want you to keep mean people from me, keep the harsh skeptics away. I don't mind the gentle skeptics because I can shepherd them, but no loud, angry people. Keep them away from me.' And they said, 'Done.' They've kept their promise, and I've been so protected. Thank you, God! And since that day in 1996, I have been teaching nonstop."

Indeed, she has. Doreen has traveled the world many times over, tirelessly teaching people how to connect with their angels for personal guidance and healing. With more than fifteen books on the subject to her credit, and because she embodies the gentleness, love, and grace attributed to the angels themselves, she has been affectionately dubbed the "Angel Lady" by fans and the media. Despite what some might assume due to her angelic bent, that Doreen might convey an "airy fairy" persona, the opposite is actually true. Dr Virtue (yes, that is her given birth name) is a remarkably well-educated woman, a doctor of psychology who holds BA, MA, and PhD degrees in counseling psychology. In fact, I learned she was the founder and former director of a psychiatric hospital for women in Tennessee and an administrator at a women's hospital in the San Francisco Bay Area. Doreen also directed three outpatient psychiatric centers, including an adolescent drug and alcohol abuse center. Despite her work in the "mainstream," Doreen believes that her ultimate purpose here on earth is to awaken people's awareness of angels—without all the religion attached to it.

"The angels are non-denominational, pure beings of Love that everybody can agree on and connect with," she says. Whether you call one a "bodhisattva" (an enlightened sentient being in Buddhism), or a god or goddess (as in Hinduism and indigenous religions), or an angel (in biblical traditions), "we are all talking about the same thing. A benevolent, unconditionally loving being who's with us spiritually at all times."

In her book, *How to Hear Your Angels*, Doreen teaches that angels bring messages from the divine mind of our Creator. The actual word "angel" means "messenger." They are gifts to us from God, sent to help us remember our divine nature, to be loving and kind, to discover and polish our talents for the betterment of the world. . . .[1] "The angels themselves," she shares with me, "are pure Love. It's all about Love, you see. Love with a capital L. You see, God is Love. And the angels are, too."

Having been raised a Protestant Christian, I hadn't heard too much about angels as a child, but my Catholic girlfriends had. They knew all about them and even claimed to have angels of their own. Doreen explains, "Everyone has at least two guardian angels, regardless of your faith, character, or lifestyle." One she describes as a "nudging angel" who pushes you to make choices in alignment with your truest self. The other is a quieter angel who comforts and lends support when you need it. Most people she has met have many angels around them at all times.

She believes our angels are with us to enact God's plan of harmony. "They help calm us, because one person at a time leads to a world of peaceful people, which equates to a world of peace. That's why our angels desire to assist us in any way that will lead to serenity."[2] And, yes, she affirms, we can actually learn to communicate with them; to hear and see them if we are openhearted and willing to try. Doreen enjoys teaching people how; her books offer detailed instructions to that end. The angels want to help, she assures me, and they are waiting for us to call upon them for guidance and personal assistance.

I spoke about this with Colleen Hughes, the editor-in-chief of *Angels on Earth*, a Guideposts publication founded by Dr. Norman Vincent Peale. Colleen confirmed what Doreen espouses. Dr. Peale himself apparently believed in angels and so did his wife. "When Dr. Peale died, in fact, Ruth had a vision of him being lifted up to heaven by the angels," says Colleen.

I had asked her if most of their contributors experienced angels in such a grandiose way. "Some do have traditional visions, but most people experience angels— 'messengers'—through simple things. Through creatures: a bird, a stray dog who shows up at exactly the right moment to touch their heart. Through found objects: a piece of music, a photograph, or a written message that lifts and inspires, changing the tone of their day.

"And then there are unexpected heroes, Good Samaritans," she said, "who come along exactly when we need them the most. The nurse who shows up at the scene of the car accident, the stranger who fixes a flat tire, the hunter who comes upon a lost and injured hiker, just in the nick of time." We are angels to one another, Colleen believes. In any given moment we can reach out to someone in kindness. We can watch over, protect, guide, and rescue one another. We can be "earth angels," thus the name of the magazine. Perceived in this light, angels take on a whole new meaning.

Despite my insightful conversations with both Colleen and Doreen, I find myself still perplexed about something. If so many of us do believe in angels, especially to protect and guide us, why does the notion of angelic contact still attract fervent naysayers? Why do people often scorn and reject those who say they have experienced them? I know from reading her candid autobiography, *The Lightworker's Way*, that Doreen has experienced such disregard herself.

Further exploration revealed to me that some people, especially those of a more conservative religious bent, fear that angels will be worshipped—that they will be venerated above God, that one might go to them for guidance instead of the Divine One itself. Doreen assures us that the angels don't want to be worshipped. In fact, she is very clear in all her writings that the glory received from their healing work or helpful presence does go to God. "Here's a gentle reminder. God is everywhere. The Divine is within you, within me, and definitely within all of the angels. . . . However, if God and the angels are one, then would it be wrong to talk directly to them? You and your angels aren't conspiring against God in some sort of mutinous plot. Aren't you merely accepting a gift that Heaven has bestowed upon you?"[3]

What is it about the mystical approach—going directly to the Source and its messengers for guidance, for assistance—that makes so many of us uncomfortable, skeptical, even judgmental of others who do so?

Carol Lee Flinders, author of *Enduring Grace: Living Portraits of Seven Women Mystics,* presents numerous women from the past who have experienced similar things—even full-blown visions of God, Jesus, Mary, and the angels. Flinders says that in the Middle Ages (when many of the women she presents as mystics in her book lived), "A chaotic, holistic, and multidimensional reality" was accepted. "Most of humankind . . . nearly all of those who lived in times past, and a great many living even now, outside industrialized society, have subscribed to that richer, multidimensional world." In fact, a belief predominated then that this richer, multidimensional world may be even "more real" than everyday reality.[1]

It was acceptable for women like Mechtild of Magdeburg or Hildegard of Bingen to have visions of and conversations with angels and other divine beings. These were often recorded for posterity. Their writings—Julian of Norwich's *Showings* and Teresa of Avila's *Interior Castle,* for example—serve as profound and accepted theological discourses for present-day seekers.

Today, I have come to understand that it is fear, housed within our ego self, that keeps us doubting the validity of such experiences. Concern, perhaps, that if we tried to connect with the upper realms, we might not be *able* to. Worry that if we opened ourselves up in this way, making ourselves vulnerable, God and emissaries may not have anything to say to us, or even abandon us in our hour of need. I maintain it is our own self-doubt that keeps us insecure enough to not even try or to negate those who do. Paralyzing self-doubt such as this keeps us at arm's length from a God who desires to be in deep communion with us in infinite ways, through infinite means.

"Instead of doubting our ability to connect with our angels," suggests Doreen, "let's look at how we already receive messages from heaven and how we can enhance that connection even more." Casting our doubts and fears aside, then, where do any of us begin to have a more communicative relationship with the Divine, especially angelic messengers? We begin by relaxing, by connecting with our sacred center, our inner temple where peace and love naturally reside. "Only the love-based higher self within each of us is able to communicate with the Divine," Doreen writes.[5]

Next, we attune ourselves to our senses—sight, hearing, touch, and smell. "Relax and breathe," she reminds us. "Don't try to make it happen." Connecting with our angels, as I understand it from Doreen's coaching, is not about forcing an experience. It is about being receptive—offering ourselves up to the Divine, being open, available, and willing. Angelic communication is very subtle, just like any communication we have with the sacred. "An emotional or physical 'feeling' is the way in which most people experience their angels."[6]

I learn from her book *How to Hear Your Angels* that for most people this is a feeling of warmth, or what may feel like a loving hug. This feeling makes you feel safe and comfortable, well-loved. It feels natural, effortless, and is accompanied by a deep knowing that "this is real." The thoughts or impressions that come through are positive, energizing, and empowering. Any messages that are conveyed are in alignment with your natural interests or talents. Sometimes, these impressions or guidance come from deceased loved ones or a sort of disembodied voice. Not to worry, says Doreen. "Hearing voices is not insanity. Many of the world's sages and saints have received guidance in the form of a disembodied voice." Also, there is often a central theme of how you can help solve a problem or help others solve theirs.[7] In the book, she provides very detailed instructions on all aspects of communicating with angels, how to discern if an angelic encounter is real, and how to interpret any messages you might receive.

There is one important point that Doreen drives home again and again as we speak. It is very important to her that we understand this. We must actually *ask* for help from the higher realms if that is what we are looking for. She explains to me that this is because we have free will, and the power of choice is a God-given one. "Though we don't ask for help often enough. We think that other people deserve help, but us? No. We think we're supposed to be strong and suffer through it. Really, we don't have to suffer. Just like we don't want our kids to suffer, our Creator doesn't want us to suffer in any way. But because we have free will, we must ask for what we want."

Hearing this, I do have one more nagging question. What about divine intervention? Is it really true that our celestial helpers can deliver us from impending disaster? "What they've told me," she explains, "is that the only time angels, guides, and/or [the] Creator can intervene in our lives is if we are in a life-endangering situation before it is our time to go." Since going public about the angelic intervention she experienced with the carjacking, Doreen has received thousands of letters

from people sharing similar experiences. "Sometimes
they hear a voice of warning, sometimes it's an angel
that incarnates as a person who saves them, and then
before the person has a chance to turn around and say
thank you, that person has disappeared. I've found that
about half the time, if the angels are trying to save you
in a life-endangering situation, they will give you very
loud, very blunt, to-the-point divine guidance. Someone
screaming at you, 'Change lanes now!' or 'Check on the
baby.'"

A reference to *Angels on Earth* after our interview
validates what Doreen has told me. I found the publication full to overflowing with stories of personal rescues,
miracles, acts of grace. And though I have not experienced a dramatic rescue such as this myself, my faith in
the higher realms to intervene when we need it most is
strong and true.

As I understand it from speaking to Doreen, angelic
brushes happen all the time, to everybody. Most are very
gentle and subtle, though—a whisper, a nudge, a wash
of love. Indeed, that is how I have experienced them
myself over the years. The Divine in any form does not
generally shout at us. It moves toward and through us
with sensations of love, peace, and joy. Always, always,
Doreen assures me, the angels' intentions and actions
are to reassure us of how much we are loved, of how
much help is available to us, and that we do not journey
through life alone. "The angels have told me that they
look past surface personality characteristics and see
the beautiful, pure light of God in each person. 'Today,
try to see yourself and others as we do . . . with love,'
they often say."[8] The angels and God perceive us in our

truest form—beautiful, holy, and whole. Wouldn't it be wonderful if we could trust and see ourselves that way!

Perhaps we can. Perhaps there is a way: by returning to the worldview we held as children. To see the world through eyes of wonder. To know that anything is possible if we simply *believe*. As children, we lived in an enchanted universe ripe with possibility. Can we remember that time and get in touch with it once again? Can we remember how wonderful it felt to live with an open heart, welcoming the day and all the magical experiences that might come our way?

Our truest self is someone who *believes* and trusts her experience. She knows what she knows and is willing to stand by it. Lately, I've been witnessing my granddaughter, Anna, in this state of discernment about what is real and what to believe. At seven, she is completely immersed in the enchantment of childhood. Yet she is also at an age when she is beginning to doubt. Everything is real—angels and fairies, Cinderella and Belle, kittens and puppies who talk— until someone tells her otherwise. When she asks me, as she often does, "Is that real?" what am I to say? What does "real" even mean? And how will my answer to her question support her magical worldview or diminish it?

When we encounter a holy woman like Doreen, we are asked to expand our reality and open ourselves up to something more—to possibilities—to ask ourselves, what is "real"? This question, serendipitously, brings us full circle, back to where our pilgrimage began many chapters ago when we were invited to uncover what we *believed*—about ourselves and our divine connection. It seems that it is time, once again, to stop, look, and listen. It is time for discernment. Time to ask that the portals of our heart be opened so we can know what is right and true for us. To listen deeply so our inner guidance can be heard. Let us ask ourselves: Do I believe in a multidimensional reality populated by celestial others? If so, do I believe God or emissaries will come to my aid or offer guidance when I need it? This is a pivotal moment for us as we determine what our level of belief and trust in the Divine actually is.

"Ultimately, it is all about Love," Doreen tells me. "That's the only thing that's going to matter. At the end of your life you are going to be asked, 'How much did you love?' That is why we are here—to remember Love."

It appears, then, that the invitation Doreen offers is the same one we have been offered by each of the guiding women we have met thus far: It is an invitation to go deeper. Go deeper into your heart and discover your unique sacred connection. Deeper into personal practices that create serenity and peace. Deeper into how you can be of service in the world. *Be angels to one another*, she says. Doreen Virtue beckons us to accept the seventh Transformational Truth, for when we do, our lives will dramatically change for the better:

I Know Divine Assistance Is Available to Me at All Times

I am grateful to Doreen for opening my eyes to new possibilities for divine connection and guidance. For challenging me to consider, once more, what it is I really believe. Speaking with her as I did, feeling her unconditionally loving regard for all of us—and for the angels—opened up a pathway in me to be more receptive to the sacred in new ways. I have become accustomed to looking for the little things that confirm the reality of angelic presence in my life—glimpses, sparkles of light, that break through on a cloudy day to restore faith and build trust. Like today . . .

As I searched for a suitable piece of inspiration to close this chapter, grace came to call, just as it had when I was struggling earlier with how to begin. Perusing my bookshelf, my eyes landed on a book a friend had given me years ago, *Peace Angels*, by Antoinette Sampson. I had not looked at it in a very long time, years perhaps, but from the tingling warmth coursing through my body, I knew that I was being urged to open its pages. Filled with stunning photography of human beings portrayed as angels, lovingly tending to other human beings, I came across these words:

> ". . . and if you search you will find
> a snapshot, a glimmer, a little hint
> of something greater than this
> And that is where I found you
> laughing and smiling
> and playing peek-a-boo.
> Oh I missed you so much.
> But I was always here, I
> never went away."[9]

My heart skipped a beat at reading the phrases. Tears welled up. I didn't know quite why, yet something urged me on. Slowly, I turned the page.

> ". . . who loved you to life?"

Suddenly, there it was. The reason for my emotional response—a photo poised right above those words. The face looking back at me was none other than my grand-mother, "Grandma D" as we called her, my father's mother. The grandmother whom I had adored, who adored me. I have missed her so much since her passing twenty-five years ago.

Tears of remembrance flowed as I felt her loving gaze upon me once more. Love wrapping itself around me in celestial embrace. How could it be, I thought, that she was here once more? I knew the photo could not possibly have been of her—or was it? It didn't really matter, though. Real or not, I was lifted up to the heavens as I read the final words on the page:

> ". . . You are never alone
> Drink your tea
> stop worrying . . ."
> *I believe.*

Reflection Questions

1. What do you believe about the existence of higher realms and the possibility of angels? About divine assistance?
2. Have you opened yourself to the possibility of being more receptive to such presence or guidance? Why or why not?
3. Have you had personal experience of divine assistance? How has this impacted your life?

Peaceful Pause

Receptivity to Divine Presence

Lie down on your back in a quiet, comfortable setting. Place your arms at your sides, palms upward, heels 6–12 inches apart. Give your body permission to open and relax into this position. Focus on the gentle movement of your in-breath and your out-breath. Allow each breath to take you deeper into feelings of peace and well-being. Continue to breathe deeply and evenly.

Now bring your attention to your heart center. Visualize a beautiful flower residing there—a rose, a lotus, any variety of many-petalled flower. Notice its vibrant color, the texture of its petals, its beautiful aroma. As you continue to breathe ever so gently, feel the breath of Spirit infusing it with life, opening your heart petal by petal. Notice all constrictions easing as you give yourself over to this beautiful sensation of opening.

Silently say to yourself:

> I open myself to you, Divine One. I let go of any preconceived notions of how I should experience you. I trust that you will reveal yourself to me in your own special way. I remain open to your revelation.

truth
eight

I Acknowledge That Difficult Times Bring Healing and Deeper Wisdom

Naomi Judd

Dawn breaks and night awakens to share secrets learned in the dark.

Kathy Sherman

Most people know her as the feisty redhead who speaks her mind and belts out songs from the heart. Her face, it seems, is everywhere. On television, she's the host of her own show, *Naomi's New Morning* on the Hallmark Channel. We may see her hosting an infomercial for her makeup line, Esteem, or being interviewed by a famous anchorperson. She is also one of the most famous mothers in America, proud mom to Wynonna, a country music powerhouse, and Ashley Judd, Hollywood actress. She's larger than life, yet a brief conversation with her confirms what I've heard all along—Naomi Judd is one of the most down-to-earth, openhearted, and caring people you'll ever meet. And she's passionate to a fault, she says, about companioning women, "as they define themselves from within."

Her story is a commonly told one: pregnant teen, abused wife, welfare mom, struggling nurse, and aspiring singer, who rose from the ashes through determination, a hefty dose of talent, and a bit of luck to become one of the most famous faces of country music. Singing duo The Judds (Naomi and daughter Wynonna) sold twenty million albums in seven years. In 1991, at the pinnacle of their phenomenal career, their reign came to an abrupt end when Naomi was forced into retirement with hepatitis C. Their "Farewell Tour" was the top-grossing act of the year. Today, Naomi is the picture of well-being after triumphing over that terminal diagnosis. She has become a celebrated author and a powerful spokesperson for health and healing, along with many other causes, including domestic violence, healthcare for women and children, and the American Liver Foundation.

I didn't meet Naomi when she was down and out, but I did meet her in later years when she had been dealt another difficult blow. It was her vulnerability that I recall bearing witness to that day, along with a display of raw courage, which endeared her to me. She made a very big impression, enough so that when the time came to write this book, I knew she absolutely must grace its pages. For that is what Naomi Judd represents to me—grace under fire. A woman who, again and again, is drawn into dark interior spaces, gleans wisdom from being there, and emerges transformed.

We met at a health exposition in Grand Rapids, Michigan. I was her opening act, so to speak. Naomi was slated to come on as the keynote speaker a few hours later. The conference was turning out to be an enormous disappointment. Though held in a very large convention center, only a dozen or so women had turned out for the opening presentation. I remember thinking, I sure hope the throngs start showing up soon, because Naomi Judd is going to be here any minute.

By the time she arrived, there were perhaps forty to fifty women seated in a grouping of three hundred chairs. The emptiness was palpable. I watched Naomi from the side of the stage, wondering how she'd react. She'd entered from the back service entrance, so she was unaware of the paltry turnout. As she stepped through the curtain wearing her best show-business smile, I saw her eyes widen, her shoulders stiffen. She faltered only for a moment, then energetically took charge. "Well, isn't this a lovely gathering," she said. "I think we should just have a nice chat, don't you, just like we're at my kitchen table back in Tennessee." With that, she stepped down from the stage and took up position on the main floor right in the middle of all those women. With that gesture, Naomi's renowned kitchen-table wisdom was in session.

But what happened next took me completely by surprise. She paused, took a deep breath, and confessed to her audience that she was not at her best this day. Her eyes filled with tears as she related her current pain, something absolutely devastating that involved her family. Truthfully, I don't remember what that revelation was. I think I must have blocked out the words, or I have conveniently forgotten them to safeguard Naomi's confession, because it was very personal. What I do remember is that I was surprised to hear it, unsure, even, why she had revealed something so intimate to us, complete strangers as we were.

And then I saw it—better yet, felt it—a display of raw courage like I've rarely experienced firsthand in another. I saw this woman rise, saw her spirit lift up before us and begin to glow with a light that was brilliant. I watched the other women notice it, too, and move their chairs in closer to her, as if they would be healed by her warmth, buoyed by her flame. It was a remarkable thing to witness. Naomi was able to set herself and her pain aside to tend to the rest of us in a deep, caring way. In that moment she became a role model of triumph over suffering for me.

After her presentation, Naomi was stationed at a table to sign copies of her candid autobiography, *Love Can Build a Bridge*. I watched again, from afar, and noticed that the strained expression I'd seen on her face earlier had returned. She looked lost in thought—a tiny, porcelain beauty awash in pain. But as soon as the first person stepped up for an autograph, the light came back on. Again, she radiated. At a break, I went over and introduced myself to her as the opening speaker. I offered her a little book of meditations I had penned, hoping it might provide some solace. "Thank you," she said graciously. "I'll tuck it in my pocketbook and read it on the plane home." I don't know if she ever did look at it. It didn't matter. In that moment, I just wanted to give her a little bit of something—a smattering of courage and hope—like she had given all of us in the audience that day.

Interviewing Naomi in 2004, I relate this story to her. She is very quiet, so quiet that I fear I have opened up an old wound for her. Her gentle response is, "I remember that day. And I remember you now. . . . Well, for me, I was in miserable pain that day. . . . But I never have gone for numbers," she says, shifting gears, referring now to the lack of attendees. "It's about heart. It's about the realness."

And that is how I find her. Despite her striking beauty and storybook existence, Naomi Judd is the real deal. As our conversation continues, I feel like I am actually sitting at her kitchen table having coffee with her, using the Four Seasons china cups and saucers she cherishes.

She tells me they were a gift, given to her when she was recovering from hepatitis C. "They mean so very much because my mother gave them to me. She was reminding me that there are seasons to life." Indeed, there are, I think to myself, and this woman has certainly had her share.

When we speak, I find her to be warm and centered. She emanates peace even over the telephone. I know that this peace has been hard won, for I have just finished her *Naomi's Breakthrough Guide: 20 Choices to Transform Your Life*. Healing for the purpose of inner peace is its recurring theme. With candor and wit, she offers personal vignettes of transformation through pain and struggle, offering sage advice for any of us who are doing the same. I am struck by her resilience, how her natural wit helps her, time and again, to access the wisdom that can be found even in tough times. She speaks of crisis: "Every crisis offers a treasure trove of information about ourselves. That's why we call it an *emergency*—you *emerge* and *see* "[1] Of making mistakes: "It's been my experience that if I learn something from a failure, then it really wasn't a mistake after all. Hey now, if you make that same mistake twice, is it a deja boo-boo?"[2] I wonder if her earthy humor is sourced in the Kentucky soil where she was born or if it is simply a natural gift, one she's honed through songwriting over the years. Either way, her cleverness works; it clarifies things and uplifts her—and us—when we seem to need it the most.

Our conversation focuses on her life-changing journey through hepatitis C, a fatal liver disease. Throughout her life, she admits, she has experienced many challenges, but this was the most terrifying by far. It was especially maddening because Naomi was, by training, a registered nurse with a long history of working within the medical community. She quickly learned traditional, allopathic medicine had no answers for her. There was no known cure for her disease. Doctors told her that she would have no more than three years to live. "All I could do was to go deep within because the outside world wasn't offering any solutions or information."

She describes how critically ill she was, confined to her bed, too weak to help herself. "When you have 'Hep C,'" as she calls it, "you feel like you have the flu, and it obviously messes with your ability to think. You don't have clarity in your thoughts, you don't have initiative. There's biochemical depression. All part of liver disease." Despite her deep desire to find answers for herself, she did not have the strength to do so. Then there were the dramatic lifestyle changes that devastated her emotionally. "The fact that I was forced to retire. And Ashley was considering moving to Hollywood because of her acting, but she didn't want to leave me. Everything that I believed and trusted and counted on all of a sudden was questioned—gone."

The darkness descended, and Naomi found herself alone in her pain, confined to bed, lost in utter despair. What she did not know in those dark moments (nor do many of us when we find ourselves in this place) was that she was being offered a profound invitation to go inside herself and connect with the Sacred One within. When we are in the midst of a dark night such as this, we often miss the unique opportunity to spend time with our soul. In fact, we usually resist it. We do not want to be in a place of discomfort or pain, so we do everything we can to move away from it. We even beg to be delivered from it, healed from it—now!—because it is such a despairing place to be. It is not in our human nature to accept periods of darkness, or to give ourselves over to their illuminating potential. However, Trappist monk Thomas Merton reminds us, "We must not refuse the providential opportunities that come to us in the midst of darkness."[3]

Naomi agrees, but she presents it a bit differently. "I think anytime that we're staring down the barrel of a forty-five we need to just really be with ourselves," she says with candor. "You hunker down. Even if that means getting in your jammies, getting under the covers, and locking your bedroom door for a while, you do it." When Naomi found herself in this place, she surrendered, held up her hands, and gave in. "What I understood was whether I liked it or not, I *was* all alone."

In that period of darkness, she found herself mulling over the words "all alone" again and again. Suddenly, she experienced a shift in awareness. It dawned on her that there could be a message here—a divine play on words. They were the words that would ultimately save her life. *All alone* became *all one*. In a moment of pure grace, Naomi realized she was not alone at all, but connected to a larger humanity, a larger energy sourced in God, that the Divine One was intimately connected with her, with everyone, even in the dark. She was given a glimpse into "All One."

From that moment on, hope floated to the surface, and she was able to begin a slow but steady search for her own cure—all from her bed. "The more clear I got about the fact that it was me and God, that I was a spiritual being having a human experience, that was all I needed. I took that first step toward self-healing."

She started reading, when energy allowed, anything and everything she could find on hepatitis C, though it was painfully slow. "I think the operable term here is 'baby steps.' I had such an insatiable curiosity to know. I sent my husband, Larry, to go buy all the books he could get his hands on. I was on such a zero-energy budget, though, I couldn't even read a whole chapter. You really do have to just say, 'Okay, this is my starting point. This is what I'm capable of doing.'" Miraculously, the information she needed to begin a healing regimen would jump right off the page in short phrases: dietary changes, supplements to take, even healing music to listen to supplied by the Evensons themselves (see "I Engage in Daily Practices That Nurture My Spirit" (pages 73–89)). The healing had begun, baby-step by baby-step.

Naomi laughingly tells me how one day she called the 800 number for the Liver Foundation for information. "I found out they didn't even have a spokesperson. I volunteered over the phone to become their spokesperson, which was pretty preposterous, because at that time I couldn't even brush my own teeth or get out of bed!" But her persistence paid off. Through hundreds of phone calls and exhaustive self-education, she did finally find "Dr. Right"—the physician who would help her create her own program for self-healing, one sourced, primarily, in alternative medicine. Miraculously, in 1995, Naomi was pronounced completely free of the hepatitis C virus. She had emerged victorious from a very dark night of the soul.

It was St. John of the Cross, a Spanish Carmelite priest from the fifteenth century, who first brought the concept of "Dark Night of the Soul" to our attention. Most of us have heard this term, and we think we understand what it means. Perhaps we have even used it ourselves to describe going through tough times. John's understanding of a dark night, however, is actually quite different from its commonplace usage. He maintained that in certain phases of our spiritual life we do experience setbacks or painful periods of disillusionment. But not all painful transitions qualify as dark nights of the soul.

Spiritual writer Thomas Moore explains, "We all have our ups and downs. At the end of struggles people sometimes claim that they have gone through an ordeal and have come out happy on the other side. One senses a degree of pride in the accomplishment. But I'm not convinced that these victories signal the kind of darkness John describes so carefully."[4]

A dark night of the soul is not about surviving, or even overcoming a difficult experience. It is about going into the depth of the experience and allowing it to lay us bare. It is not about triumph or finding solutions to our problems. Instead, it is about following the divine thread which leads down into our soul's core to where there are actually no answers at all. There is nothing, only emptiness, and resting there in that emptiness. "The dark night," writes Mirabai Starr, a translator of John of the Cross's writings, "is not an abstract notion on some list of spiritual experiences every seeker is supposed to have. The dark night descends on a soul only when everything else has failed."[5]

This is precisely what happened to Naomi. In a pivotal moment of darkness, feeling completely alone, she moved into a place of inner emptiness—of silence. This is a choiceless choice when we can do nothing else but surrender. It is in this vast, eternal silence that we hear it, says John. We hear God's voice. Naomi heard it.

For her, "Alone" became "All One." "God is here," the voice said, "even in this dark place." This awareness, says John, is the beginning of blessedness.

What happens next is truly an act of grace. Love swoops in, God Love with a capital L. The emptiness we were experiencing is replaced by Love, and we find ourselves transformed. Not only do we change in that split-second moment of blessing, we become an entirely new person.

After Naomi's dark night, not only did she begin to heal from a life-threatening illness, but her entire worldview changed. She believes she was given a new life's purpose: helping others heal and thrive. She also created a vibrant new lifestyle for herself, one focused on personal peace and body-mind-spirit wellness. Today, she is considered to be one of the most vocal proponents of alternative healing. The reality is if it had not been for hepatitis C and the dark night brought on by that diagnosis, she would not likely be the woman she is today.

When the Spirit (in collaboration with our own spirit) determines that it's time for any of us to mature spiritually, to grow into a brighter version of ourselves, a wake-up call is often issued. We are given a bold shove into new awareness through a loss or life crisis. It is up to us in that moment of crisis to discern what it is that is happening to us, to decipher what this particular opportunity is all about and find meaning in it. Ram Dass, one of the most gifted spiritual teachers of our day, may have described this process best in *Still Here*, his own account of a dark night of the soul, his dealing with the life-changing effects of a debilitating stroke. "Healing is not the same as curing," he said. "Healing does not mean going back to the way things were before but rather allowing *what is now* to move us closer to God."[6]

A dark night of the soul is actually a potentially fertile time, a divinely issued invitation to move deeper into the heart of God—if we can see it as that. In 2002–2003, life presented me with a dramatic series of wake-up calls, one precariously stacked upon the other like the poorly written lyrics of a country western song. My ailing twenty-four-year marriage finally disintegrated, followed by a gut-wrenching divorce. I found myself absolutely broke. My son dropped out of high school. My oldest daughter joined the Marine Corps and was shipped off to Iraq. My father was dying of cancer. At the time, I had no idea any invitation at all was being offered. It felt to me as if my life had completely fallen apart, and I didn't have a clue how to put it back together.

One day, while sitting in my spiritual direction training program (one of the few bright lights in my life at the time), I was consumed with pain at the horrific turn my life had taken. Tears were so close to the surface that I didn't dare speak. At a break, one of my teachers who had sensed my emotional state, Michael Fonseca, came over to me and said, "Let's take a walk."

As we strolled the corridor, in a gentle tone he queried, "Do you know what is happening to you?" I shook my head silently— *No*. "You are being purified," he said. "Do you know what that means?" Again— *No*. In the next few minutes, Michael spelled out for me how purification worked. There may come a time in one's spiritual life when the Divine One calls us home to our truest self. This is done by a series of acts, a stripping away, peeling back the layers of the false self. We are being asked to let go of everything that we are attached to that keeps us separated from the heart and mind of God.

By clarifying my journey, Michael opened the door for me to consciously enter into that dark night and surrender to its curative power. To be in a place of emptiness with no answers. To listen to the divine voice which could guide me forward. Surrendering to a transformational process such as this was not a matter of choice for me. It was an act of engagement, as Ram Dass described—allowing *what is now* to move me closer to God. Thankfully, lessons were learned in the dark, and I was ultimately transformed. In fact, most of what fills this book is a result of that profound conversion. Without that dark night, I would not be who I am today.

As Naomi herself attests, the lessons we learn in this time of spiritual darkness spill over into all areas of our lives. "I think that living in the moment was one of the first, most profound lessons I learned, because when you feel so darn crummy, you really can't do anything else. I was just flattened with Hep C. I couldn't be 'out there' in the world; I had to be 'in here,'" indicating her interior self.

She explains how going from the "macrocosm to the microcosm" changed her dramatically. "Previous to my illness, I was so overstimulated. Being an entertainer, I was going from city to city every night. I designed our outfits, wrote the songs, and put together the set sheets. When I became ill, I began to understand that everything that really matters is in here, in me, where I am in this very moment." She describes to me how she became acutely appreciative of everything—sounds, sights, smells, even relationships. "I was able to begin to be completely present to the person I was with."

I think to myself, *yes*, that is what I witnessed in Naomi that day at the health expo—her ability to be completely present to someone, even if she didn't know them intimately, like the women in the audience, like myself. This gift of being present to others came only after she had learned to become present to herself in the midst of her own suffering—to be fine with what *is*. She describes how everyday occurrences continue to bring her back to what is important for her now—to be fully awake in the present moment.

"I remember going to Vanderbilt Hospital in Nashville to get some blood drawn, and I wound up praying with people. Strangers who were sitting there in wheelchairs with hospital bracelets on, with IVs, and it was very humbling, very gratifying. I was talking to the phlebotomist whose daughter had gotten into trouble the night before, and here I am—I can barely walk back and forth to my car—witnessing and hugging him while he's drawing my blood. That's when you realize that life is completely unpredictable. When you can go with what I now call 'Whatever Happens,' it's wonderful! There is no agenda. Life is an ebb and flow."

Everywhere Naomi goes now it seems people want to talk to her about healing. "I do get in a pickle sometimes when people approach me on the street and want some silver bullet. I'm grateful now that I've got my book. In fact, I carry a carton of them in the trunk of my car. I was at the car wash yesterday, and someone asked me a question. I said, 'Okay, follow me out to the car,' and I'm passing them out like some sort of . . . oh, well. Wynonna now calls me a 'musicianary,'" she laughs.

As I listen to Naomi tell her stories about how her life is so very different now, I am deeply touched by the

passion she has for her spiritual journey and her ongoing commitment to supporting the growth journeys of
others. I am reminded how important it is for us to be
fully conscious—wide awake—so that we can attend to
our spiritual lives and then help others to do the same.
By surrendering to our own dark nights, our truest self
will rise up like a bright beacon. We will be made new, as
will our relationship with the Divine, if we stay faithful
to the process. Naomi Judd, by her excellent example,
has shown us the value of the eighth Transformational
Truth:

I Acknowledge That Difficult
Times Bring Healing
and Deeper Wisdom

This truly is our life's calling. To be a willing par-
ticipant in our sacred unfoldment, no matter the price,
no matter how difficult. The dark night of the soul is
ultimately about freedom—inner freedom—to live as
our truest selves in God for all the world to see.

Today, I am newly appreciative of Naomi's kitchen-
table wisdom, this compendium of secrets learned in
the dark. "I know that you understand what I'm saying,
Jan, because you have been through something similar.
But it's really hard for somebody who hasn't been on the
edge of the cliff to know that sometimes the worst stuff
that happens to us provides the greatest growth."

"The more I am exposed to the complexities of life,"
she says, "the simpler it gets for me. This morning, for
example, I go downstairs and there sits this sweet, little
old man, my husband's uncle George. And he's just

sitting in awe looking at my garden. He tells me he set his alarm for 6:00 a.m. so that he could get up and watch the morning glories open. I have a healing garden with bird feeders and a fountain and statues. I have a mirror ball, and how corny and glitzy are they?" she laughs. "I am just so grateful for my world . . ."

~~~

As I put the finishing touches on this chapter, I decided to visit Naomi's website one more time to see if there were any details I should add to the text. I checked her appearance schedule, wondering if she might, by chance, perform again. I was surprised to find that in May 2008 she and Wynonna are planning to offer a reunion concert. My heart did a little dance of celebration for her, because I know what that means—she has fully recovered— her whole and holy self. I was curious, though, what her singing voice might sound like, if it will have changed after all these years. I imagine that it has, for she herself has shifted and changed. Naomi Judd sings a different tune today—one of healing and hope for all of us who struggle, as she has.

"In the landscape of the soul there is a desert, a wilderness, an emptiness," wrote Ray Faraday Nelson, "and all great singers must cross this desert to reach the beginning of their road. Jesus. Buddha. Mohammed. All wandered through the wasteland, speaking to demons, speaking to empty air, listening to the wind, before finding their dove, their bo tree, their stone tablets, before finding their true voice."

Naomi Judd, it seems, has found hers.

Reflection Questions

1. Have you experienced a dark night of the soul? If so, how did it transform you and your life? What have you learned?
2. How would you characterize your ability to "let go and let God"?
3. How have any dark nights you may have experienced changed your relationship with the Divine?

Peaceful Pause

Surrendering to Change

(Best done outdoors in a quiet, private place)

Take a deep breath and plant yourself in the midst of Mother Nature's beauty. Take another breath to settle more deeply into your surroundings. Gently take note of what you see all around you. Note the temperature, the sky, grass, flowers, trees—all the manifestations of nature. Note all the changes that are taking place in nature right now, all going on around you. Continue breathing gently and easily, settling into your body in this beautiful setting.

Like all living things in nature, we, too, are being asked to change. To release something that no longer serves our highest good—a trait, an attitude, behavior, or relationship. Select something you wish to release. Next, raise your arms so they are parallel to the ground, palms up. Imagine the something you have chosen to release is now sitting in the palms of your hands. Give it a shape, color, and texture.

Now close your eyes and imagine it being easily carried away by gentle winds to new terrain. Watching it float away, say to yourself:

> I let go of all that restricts me. I release it to the Universe. I surrender to the winds of change. I am grateful for this opportunity to let go so that I can expand and grow into my truest self in God.

truth
nine

I Can Create My Life Anew Each Day

Michelle Tsosie Sisneros

Today, like every other day, we wake up empty and frightened. Don't open the door to the study and begin reading. Take down a musical instrument. Let the beauty we love be what we do.

Jalaluddin Rumi

We were surrounded by beauty, soulful renderings of heart and hand. Earth-hued pottery, turquoise-encrusted jewelry, and colorfully woven rugs offered a feast for the senses. We were in our element, my sister Linda and I, wandering through a delightful maze of Mother Earth–inspired creativity. It was 2000, and we delightedly found ourselves at the annual Native American art show held at the Museum of Man in San Diego, California.

Years earlier, Linda had introduced me to her passion, collecting Native American art. It was an affection that so enraptured her that, in time, she became a representative of indigenous artists' work. Her joy in doing so rubbed off on me, and I had become a collector as well. We vowed to always make our purchases from the artists themselves to ensure they would be paid fairly for their offerings. Our buying trips took us into the heart of "Indian country," meeting face to face with some of the finest artists in the world. These companionable journeys to Taos, Sante Fe, Canyon de Chelly, and First

Mesa allowed our sisterly connection to deepen in wonderful ways.

It was this newfound sense of sisterhood that led us to the booth of artist Michelle Tsosie Sisneros. From across the room I spotted her drawings, unique renderings of women in communion with one another. Her style of painting was simple, but innovative.

The artist, who stood proudly beside her work, was strikingly beautiful, a Native American woman in her forties, I guessed, with medium-brown skin and long, dark hair. What struck me the most about her, though, was her confidence of bearing combined with genuine warmth and an openhearted spirit that invited us into her space without the use of words. When she did talk, she was gentle of speech, yet passionate about her work. Her sacred presence drew us in, and before we knew it, Linda and I were chatting happily with Michelle about her art.

My attention was drawn to one work in particular, a depiction of four women in a queue, arms around each other's waists. Only their backs were visible, which lent to the mystery of the piece, because there were no faces to convey mood or emotion. Yet, somehow, you could feel the love and affection for one another flowing between them. I picked up the print and turned it over. On the back was one word: "Sisters." I felt the familiar fluttering of Spirit touch my heart; my eyes filled with tears as my gaze moved to my own sister, who had come to mean so much to me.

Linda was lost in conversation with Michelle, but she must have felt my eyes upon her as she quickly turned around and glanced down at the picture I held in my hands. I passed it over to Linda. She looked at it carefully, only to have the same tearful response I had. With the simplicity of her sketched figures and a well-placed word, Michelle had captured the essence of what it meant to be a true sister to someone, and we were both amazed.

Noticing our emotional response, Michelle reached into a box lying on the table and produced the story behind the original painting. Together, Linda and I read:

> I am grateful to the Creator for the gift of my sister. She has made my life as a woman richer. Her life has mirrored mine in so many ways that I am the student to her in life. This has given me the deepest respect for her. I have come to find through the years, whatever hurts and pains that have followed us are no longer. We are close and loving, women, friends, family, and sisters. I am grateful and humbled for the gift of sisterhood.

Sisterly tears continued to flow and we found ourselves saying simultaneously, "I'll buy one for you for your birthday!" We dissolved into laughter at that joint pronouncement and made our purchases. Michelle and Linda agreed to connect about doing business together in the future, and we moved on.

Over the next few years, my sister stayed in touch with Michelle, often meeting up with her at art shows throughout the Southwest. I learned that she lived a solitudinous life at Santa Clara Pueblo in New Mexico. Naturally, when the time came to gather interviews for this book, I thought of Michelle, as my first impression was that she had embodied her truest self. (This was confirmed for me when we met again in Sante Fe a few years later.) I found myself wondering what her daily life in the Pueblo might be like and how it would support her ability to live in a sacred manner. I naively assumed that doing so would be a simple thing for her. I envisioned Michelle being immersed in Native American ways that breathed sanctity and fostered divine connection.

Within the first few minutes of our telephone conversation I learn that she grew up without any knowledge of her spiritual heritage. "I am a Santa Clara/Navajo/ Laguna/Mission Indian woman," she begins. "I grew up on the Navajo-Dineh reservation. The land was long and far in between the people living there. I have strong memories of growing up feeling very alone. I came from an alcoholic family, and my father was a closed man about his childhood and upbringing. I grew up in the Catholic religion, but had no understanding of spirituality from it.

"I had family in Santa Clara Pueblo, though, and was able to participate in activities there that gave me some understanding of Native spirituality, and also through my mother's Pueblo—Laguna Pueblo. I longed to be in Santa Clara, though, where I eventually married, and raised my son. I believe I am tied to the earth here."

I am surprised at her revelation and at the same time dismayed at my own false assumption that because she is a Native American woman she would naturally, by virtue of her heritage, be spiritually inclined. As Michelle's story unfolds, I discover that, like most of us, she had to choose her connection to Spirit, give birth to it, then nurture it to life.

She continues to share. "You see, becoming a more spiritually aware person started for me late in life—since I went to treatment for alcohol and drug addiction."

Another stunning revelation. I truly had no idea Michelle had struggled with something like this. Our conversation feels all too synchronistic because, in this very moment, I am walking through addiction with a dear loved one myself. It is a tempestuous journey for us, one for which, on most days, I feel ill-prepared. I find myself remaining silent about this though, as I want to focus, heart and soul, on her journey and provide sacred space for the telling of her tale. Waiting upon her words, I breathe in a prayer of clarity and understanding for us both.

"I'm forty-eight years old now, and for thirty-eight years of my life I disrespected myself. I have lived life as it can be most disrespected. And now I am finding out how to live life at its fullest. It all began when I was a kid. . . ."

Without offering too many details, Michelle describes growing up in a dysfunctional family, riddled with alcoholism and domestic violence. She and her brother, fourteen months younger, were close, inseparable, as often happens among siblings in dysfunctional families. In mid-childhood they became drinking buddies and, later, drug users together. In adulthood they remained close, even descending into alcoholism together.

"He ended up dying from alcoholism. He locked himself up in his house and drank himself to death. You see, I had gone into recovery, and he just couldn't, so it caused a distance between us that was heart-wrenching because we had been so very close all our lives. In the final days of his life, he let me back in, though. I was the only person he wanted to see. I rode with him in the ambulance to the hospital, and we talked and made amends. We found our peace."

I wonder why it is that Michelle was able to break free of alcoholism and her brother was not. She answers my question candidly, "At one point, I just got really tired of the disrespect I'd brought upon myself. I had hurt so many people in my life because of my addiction, especially my son. I could tell you story after story. I sit back and think, 'Oh, my God, I did the things to him that my father did to me.' Things I swore I wouldn't do to my own children, and probably worse."

As Michelle speaks, I find myself journeying back in time with her, mentally witnessing images of a woman spiraling out of control, a woman inflicting pain on those she loves because she had been so very hurt herself. I silently weep for her and her loved ones. I don't trust my emotion-filled voice, so I stay quiet and let her continue to weave her story.

"So, I went into treatment, but I did it for all the wrong reasons. To save my relationship with my husband, with my son, not for myself. Treatment isn't one of those cloud-nine things where you go in and come out and life's great. It got worse when I came home. I still have days when I think, 'Oh, God, when are these amends ever going to end?' I realize that you don't go along for almost thirty-eight years of your life hurting people and not have a lot of amends to make . . ."

I'm aware that Michelle is now referring to steps eight and nine of the Twelve Steps of Alcoholics Anonymous, the program of recovery that worked for her: "Make a list of all persons we had harmed, and become willing to make amends to all . . . then make direct amends to these people wherever possible." I know this only because I have recently read these words myself in the pages of the books I go to daily to better understand my own loved one's journey of recovery. I wonder when he, like Michelle, will come to a place where he can begin to make amends of his own.

"I do believe that my faith in the Creator played a big part in me seeing the light. And I know I have inner strength, which I must have gotten from my mother, who is a strong woman. I also believe in miracles. There have been so many miracles in my life, especially with my son. He's twenty-four now, and I have a little grand-son. It's been a long, hard road being a mother, and I still have a long way to go, but it's getting easier, and it's actually getting to be fun and loving and peaceful. My son and I have done much healing together. The fact that we have now come to a place that we are as loving as a mother and son can be is a miracle."

As Michelle speaks, she is calm and centered, which tells me she has arrived on the other side of her pain. She clearly remembers the past and has taken full respon-sibility for her life and her choices, which is precisely why I consider her to be a fully embodied holy woman. Despite her past, despite what happened to her as a child, and the disempowering choices she once made for herself as an adult, she remains committed to her healing journey. Her passion for it is strong, evidenced in the whole and holy life she has created for herself at Santa Clara Pueblo.

But what did Michelle do to get there? What steps did she take to reclaim herself and her life, to free herself from the clutches of addiction?

By her own admission, she began with an honest assessment. She noticed how she was getting hooked into negative behavior and the damage it was causing in her life. She realized how her addiction was holding her back from feeling joy and inner peace, from having loving relationships, even doing meaningful work, all things sourced in her most sacred self, a self she was not able to access while addicted.

Gerald May, MD, wrote about this process of recovering our sacred selves in his book *Addiction and Grace*. He reminds us that *every single one of us has addictions*. Addictions can be described as compulsions, preoccupations, or attachments covering a wide variety of human behaviors. Many of us are addicted to substances that temporarily make us feel better: nicotine, alcohol, drugs, sugar, caffeine, and chocolate, to name a few. Or we are addicted to things: television, money, status, food, exercise, sex, work. All of us, however, are addicted to behaviors: achievement, spending, being in control, having responsibility, sexual intimacy, eating, being liked, being the victim, helping others, and many more.[1]

May goes on to explain that any addiction, compulsion, or attachment sidetracks us and dims the energy of our deepest desires for love and goodness.[2] In other words, it keeps us separated from our true identity and our innate desire to live in harmony with the Spirit. Addiction keeps us looking in the wrong direction— outside of ourselves for validation, for pleasure, for relief. Our thoughts, emotions, and behaviors become acutely focused on the people, objects, or situations that we believe will help us feel better about ourselves in the moment. We fail to see (because of the nature of the addiction itself) that the "fix" is false, providing only temporary relief, and the cycle of craving, desiring, and enacting begins all over again.

Our addictions, no matter what they are, will always keep us disconnected from our truest selves. If we are to become the luminous women we were born to be, we need to be truthful about the light and the dark of us—to notice where our attention is focused, what preoccupies us, what drives us, what serves as a compulsion to lure us away from God, and what prevents us from living as our most divine self. Our recovery at this point in our journey then becomes not only about recovering from addiction, but about *recovering our whole and holy self*, one that, until now, may have been forgotten or buried beneath decades of emotional pain.

Michelle's soul-baring honesty about her addiction and how she chose to transform it invites us to look at our own addictions. In the spirit of healing and wholeness, let us candidly ask ourselves: What is it I am personally addicted to? What behaviors preoccupy my thinking and choice-making? What desires and behaviors hold me back from being my truest self?

Since my eye-opening conversation with Michelle, I have been continually invited to look at my addictions, to assess them openly and honestly, and to boldly admit how they might keep me disconnected from my truest self. It does take courage to peel back the layers of our false selves, but it is an effort that is absolutely necessary. If we don't or can't, we will continue to remain small, ineffectual, fragmented versions of ourselves.

Recognizing my desire to please and be liked by others has been one such realization of an addiction. This often played itself out as insecurity when I spoke aloud to others, from providing an answer in a class I was taking to offering an opinion in casual conversation. After the fact, I would find myself hand-wringing with worry about what I'd said, second-guessing myself by wondering how I might have expressed myself better. I was concerned about what others would think of me because of what I had said.

I realized, in time, that my addiction to being liked was manifesting in other sorts of behaviors: excessive gift giving, complimenting when I didn't mean it, saying yes and over-volunteering, and agreeing with others to avoid conflict. The result of my addiction was an extremely self-conscious woman who was a mere shadow of her holy woman self.

To heal from this addiction of being liked has been a journey of many years. The key to my recovery, as it is for any of us, was to honestly assess what was holding me back from being my truest self. Then I made whole-some new choices for myself.

We begin the journey of re-creating our lives one choice at a time by determining if that choice will bring us into greater alignment with our sacred selves or take us further away. We take our next step based on this determination, then another. When life offers up certain situations, we strive to be keenly aware of whether each choice we make is leading us into the heart of our sacred selves—or not.

Let us remember that at this point in the recovery of our truest selves, all that we can do may be to take one step. We take one step at a time—and that has to be enough. We are enough. We are healing, recovering. We cannot possibly see from this vantage point a long-term, clear-cut path for ourselves. We must remain in the present moment and listen, watch, and choose the next divinely revealed step.

As human beings, we have been given free will. Free will enables us to make the appropriate choices that release us from the stranglehold of our compulsions and addictions. But we must exercise our free will with perseverance, heartfelt desire, and passion for ourselves—as women who deserve to live free. The poet Rumi's advice rings true on this one: "Halfheartedness doesn't reach into majesty. You set out to find God, but then you keep stopping for long periods at meanspirited roadhouses." For without commitment and passion for our own healing journey, we will be drawn back into the meanspirited roadhouses of which Rumi speaks, patterns of addictive behavior that will inevitably, by their very nature, lure us back into lesser ways of being. Vigilance, tempered with self-compassion, is vital to recovering our sacred selves. Minute by minute, hour by hour, we must be our own loving champions, fully aware that a particular thought, feeling, or action could bring us closer to Spirit or take us further away.

We must also remember that the journey to reclaiming our sacred selves is one that is rooted in profound faith. Once we have made the commitment to move forward, we trust that we will be shown the next step to take, and the next one after that, and the next one after that. Doing so allows us to surrender to the process of our own unfolding.

But what, you may ask, if choice-making isn't enough? What if we just can't seem to garner the strength or the courage to say no to our addictions and yes to new life? What then?

We pray. We ask for help. We throw ourselves on the mercy of the Universe, God, the Great Spirit, the All—by whatever name we call the Divine—and we ask for guidance. We expect and wait for it to arrive. We open ourselves to grace.

Gerald May concurs. In *Addiction and Grace*, he writes, "Because of our addictions, we simply cannot—on our own—keep the great commandments. Most of us have tried, again and again, and failed. . . . I think our failure is necessary, for it is in failure and helplessness that we can most honestly and completely turn to grace. Grace is our only hope in dealing with addiction, the only power that can truly vanquish its destructiveness."[3]

As a doctor and therapist, May attests that grace is real. He has witnessed its healing power over and over again in his private practice with his patients. In fact, in informal surveys he conducted with recovering addicts, they reported that what helped them turn their lives around was having a spiritual experience of some sort. May reports that they all seemed to turn to God (however they perceive him/her/it) at some juncture of their recoveries. They attribute their healing to a profound personal experience.

Michelle, too, vouches for the healing power of grace. "I believe my art is a gift from God, and it saved me. I can't explain where it came from or why I have it. I've never been to an art class; I've never studied under another artist. All I know is that as a child I loved to draw. It was a relief from my crazy childhood. Drawing was therapeutic for me, but when my life began to take a self-destructive turn, my drawing left me."

She explains that a few years after she completed her drug and alcohol treatment program, she started to wonder what it would be like to draw again. She would sit at her desk at her office job, noticing that she had picked up a pencil and had begun to draw like in the past. "I started to wish that I could be home, just drawing and painting, though I had no idea how I could possibly make a living doing that. I hadn't thought about my art in years, and I was really rusty."

Michelle mentioned her desire to pursue her art to her then-fiancé (now her husband), Murphy, and he encouraged her to quit her job and make a commitment to it. He even volunteered to support her financially so that she could. "So, I went for it," she says. "And I hadn't painted in years. I had no idea of what style I would start out in or how I was going to do any of this. The first couple of years, I was really unhappy with my work.

"But then my brother died, the one I spoke about earlier, the brother I was so close to all my life. He started coming to me in very spiritual dreams. I believe he was encouraging me not to give up my art, but to persevere. Then, certain things began to change. I started to find focus for my work, and the skill of my drawing improved." In other words, grace happened.

The result was the painting "Sisters," the same one Linda and I purchased in San Diego all those years before. Michelle's work expanded from there, and today she is an award-winning artist and illustrator, whose work has been showcased all over the country. "I've taken my innate ability to draw and paint and just gone with it. I now paint from my soul. For that reason alone, I know the Creator really does bestow miracles upon people."

In her book *The Artist's Way*, artist Julia Cameron testifies to a similar journey of grace and redemption from her addiction of alcoholism. She writes, "I learned to turn my creativity over to the only god I could believe in, the god of creativity." Her landmark book is a guided journey in making the connection between one's creativity and one's spirituality. Creative expression is not simply about being an artist of some medium, she maintains. It is about allowing the Divine to flow through you so you can experience the most complete version of yourself that you can be. "Our creative dreams and yearnings come from a divine source. As we move toward our dreams, we move toward our divinity."[4]

The brush strokes that are placed upon the canvas and the poetry that finds its way to paper afterward, Michelle affirms, come in and through God. They are conjoined efforts, human and Divine—gift, honed skill, and inspiration all blended into one soulful endeavor, as is all of our creative expression when it is done with love and passion. Religious thinker and visionary Matthew Fox concurs that connecting with our innate gifts, our creativity, and our passion can reconnect us to our sacred selves: "Creativity is not a noun or even a verb—it is a place, a space, a gathering, a union, a where—wherein the Divine powers of creativity and human power of imagination join forces. Where the two come together is where beauty and grace happens, and, indeed, explodes."[5]

It is our unique creative expression, whatever that might be—child rearing, gardening, social activism, teaching, singing, healing arts, even daily work—done with passion and commitment that can deliver us to our holy woman selves. It is creative expression, Fox claims, that is truly the medicine we need for our addictions. He proposes that most addictions come from surrendering

our own real powers—our powers of creativity. "We
get a temporary 'high' from some external stimulus, be
it nicotine or sugar, speed or acid, sex or more money,
entertainment or television—and that is our sad substi-
tute for the joy and ecstasy of creativity and creation. . . .
If we were creative, would we be so addicted? If we are
addicted, can we be creative?"[6]

These are powerful questions, ones that each of us
must answer for ourselves. In the spirit of growth, I
pose them to you here: What is your unique creative
expression? What is your personal magic, your gift,
your talent? Have you connected with it yet, and are
you living and breathing it? Connecting with our unique
creative expression can open the door to the Sacred One
within.

By the very testament of her life, Michelle demonstrates how this process works, how anyone can
overcome her history and adversity by making healthy
new choices for herself. By honoring the creative spirit
within her, Michelle was delivered from the clutches
of addiction and placed in the lap of the ever-loving
Divine. She has transformed her life, one choice at a
time. It is a heroine's journey, one that every single one
of us is called to take if we are to live deeply meaningful
lives. Michelle Tsosie Sisneros embodies for us the ninth
Transformational Truth:

I Can Create My Life Anew
Each Day

With the dawn of each new day comes many choices
about who we wish to be and how we can live. Are we

willing to let go of anything that keeps us from becoming intimate with our truest selves? Release whatever prevents us from connecting with the Divine One within? Today can be the day we begin again, to rededicate our lives and reorient ourselves toward Spirit. Rest assured, the golden opportunity of a life sourced in the Spirit awaits us, choice by faith-filled choice, as surely as the sun rises in the sky each day.

~~~

This morning at first light, I rose and walked outside to breathe in the fresh morning air and give thanks for the day ahead. I thought of Michelle, a true sister of my soul, and aligned my spirit with hers. I saw her in my mind's eye, standing outside her home in the Pueblo facing east. She greets the sun and scatters cornmeal to thank Mother Earth. It is her most special moment of the day, she says, when she is alone and the whole world is asleep. Then she begins to pray. She prays for her children and grandchildren. For her family and friends. For all the people in her pueblo and everything around them. She calls this her "Native Prayer."

"As my day goes on," Michelle tells me, "I find myself praying all day. I pray for the people in Iraq, for the children all over the world who have no water. I think about all the women who are so angry, who are very sad or beaten. I pray for people who are ill. At times, I still find myself saying the 'Our Father' and the 'Hail Mary,' and I light candles. I keep my medicine pouch around me all the time, and I have the medicine man make little bundles for my grandkids. That is how I pray."

And she paints. Painting is her prayer, too. Her thoughts, words, and daily actions, carefully chosen, are stanzas of unspoken prayer. In fact, her entire life is a prayer, a sacred offering of her whole and holy self to the Divine One who lives and breathes in her. As it can be for each of us . . .

As I stood outside my own house in northern Michigan, the sun kissing my face on a warm spring morning, my prayer floated through the heavens to join with hers from the dusty flats of New Mexico. We prayed for all of us. We prayed to remember who we are—holy women— by birth and destiny. We prayed for the strength and courage it will take for our journeys home to our truest selves in God, journeys not unlike the Long Walk Michelle's ancestors, the Navajo people, the Dineh, took more than a century ago.

"Gods of the afterlife," I imagine her praying, "priests of the stars, watch over us. Bring me dreams of my ancestors and lead me to a place of good, kind heart."[7]

And I prayed in turn, "I am grateful to the Creator for the gift of this new sister. She has made my life as a woman richer."

Reflection Questions

1. What addictions/compulsions might be preventing you from living as your truest self? Have you attempted to release these and/or recover from them?
2. What actions could you take today to create a new tomorrow for yourself?
3. What creative spark, gift, or talent would like to be ignited in you?

Peaceful Pause

New Beginnings

Close your eyes and take in a deep, cleansing breath. Allow this breath, the breath of the Spirit, to move through you like a gentle wind that clears a room full of stagnant air. Feel this cleansing Spirit-breath move tenderly through you. Feel it flow, from head to toe, with soft, sweeping rhythm, clearing out dusty spaces, cobwebs, stuffiness. Welcome this cool breeze into all the passageways of your body, mind, and heart. Feel it flow. . .

Continue to inhale and exhale, slowly, evenly, one sweeping breath after another. Breathe out, sweep out stagnation. Breathe in, sweep in freshness. Out with the old; in with the new. Imagine all of your inner windows and doors flung wide open to this cleansing Spirit-wind. Letting out old ways of being that no longer serve. Letting in vital new energy.

Notice how much cleaner you feel now. How much lighter and brighter you feel. It is a brand-new day and anything is possible. Breathe in new life for yourself, then see yourself taking the first steps toward living this day as your truest self.

truth
ten

I Trust the Divine Timing
of My Own Unfolding

Joan Borysenko

Just remain in the center, watching.
And then forget that you are there.

Lao Tzu

We pride ourselves on knowledge, on being able to find the answers to life's burning questions. Being a teacher by training and an ardent learner, I believed that if I searched hard and long enough, I'd eventually acquire all the answers I needed. There comes a time, however, in every holy woman's journey when, no matter the depth or breadth of our search, there are absolutely no answers to be found. Despite all our efforts and deep desire to know, we discover that our orderly universe—and our individual lives—are full of gaping holes, ripe with mystery.

Many years ago, bogged down in my own unanswered questions—especially the "why" of things—I came across the book *Letters to a Young Poet* by Rainer Maria Rilke. His advice-giving missives, penned to a fellow poet younger than himself, were intriguing. It seemed as if he were speaking directly to me. "You are so young; you stand before beginnings," said Rilke. "I would like to beg of you, dear friend, as well as I can, to have patience with everything that remains unsolved in your heart." That's asking a lot, I thought to myself, especially from someone who is sorely lacking in patience. I was so bereft of this virtue, in fact, that I habitually wore a baseball cap with the Chinese symbol for patience on the front, its English translation written on the back. I thought if I wore it often enough, perhaps those characters—"Patience"— might sink into me by osmosis.

Then Rilke went on to make an even more daunting request of his young poet friend . . . and of me: "Try to love the *questions themselves*, like locked rooms and like books written in a foreign language. Do not look now for the answers," he advised. "They cannot now be given to you because you could not live them. It is a question of experiencing everything. At present you need to *live* the question."[1]

For a passionate searcher, to *not* seek answers to questions? That is an impossibility, I thought. That's like asking a human being not to breathe, or sleep, or eat! But ask, Rilke did, and by some glimmer of grace, I stopped resisting and vowed to be a good pupil on this one. I knew he was right. It was time for me to live my questions.

Rilke was not the only mentor at this time who invited me to let go of "knowing," to surrender into life as it was—uncertain and mysterious—and to be all right with that. Joan Borysenko, author and scientist, became my other mentor. I'd read many of her books and found her approach to life fascinating. A scientist by training, she was passionate about seeking and finding answers. She still is. Yet somewhere along the way she dropped down into a deeper part of herself and began to live the questions, even love the questions, embracing the enigma of life.

It was Joan's book *A Woman's Journey to God* that demonstrated to me her ability to live fully, vibrantly, with paradox. I was enamored with her spiritual journey and how she had learned to become comfortable with uncertainty. I had the opportunity to finally ask her about her journey in 2004. In two lengthy conversations, we traveled the length and breadth of her spiritual journey. What I've come to learn, with Joan's assistance, is how *not* knowing can actually take us into deeper communion with the Mystery—and into our sacred self.

The Mystery, I believe, can hold two meanings simultaneously (another paradox). It is a reference to the Divine One—G-D, as the Hebrew people called it, or the Unknowable, the I Am presence, in other traditions. At the same time, it also refers to the sacred process of life itself, a process that is mysteriously sourced in holiness, one that we cannot make rational sense of, no matter how hard we try. Life as Mystery is a process to be engaged rather than figured out.

Joan's relationship with the Mystery and the questions surrounding it began as a young girl while sitting on her father's lap. "He was such a beloved father and friend," she tells me. "He had the capacity to make his index finger and his middle finger buzz past each other. It would sound like a bee. I remember that he buzzed his fingers around and came to rest on my belly button. He said, 'If God is really a man with a white beard sitting up in the sky, and I was an airplane, my fingers would go right through God's belly button. Do you really think that's what God is?'"

As Joan describes it, this is her father's first spiritual teaching to her. "It was wonderful because he was telling me that you have to think, you have to love the question. You have to engage what is God. You can't just say, 'Well,

I was told God is a person with a white beard.' It was an awakening experience for me at five or six years old."

Shortly after that she remembers entering into a phase of wondering what life was all about. "'Where could we come from? How does something come out of nothing? What was there before nothing?' I had this wonderful bedroom with big windows, and I would often see the moon outside my window. I would go to sleep contemplating those kinds of questions."

Joan's parents were secular Jews and agnostic. Her father, a great influence on her life, was a "nature mystic," as she describes him, in the vein of Emerson and Thoreau. Her mother was more concerned with the realities of anti-Semitism. Both were first-generation Jewish-Americans, their families having left the pogroms of eastern Europe before the onset of World War II.

At age eight, Joan found herself sent to a Jewish summer camp because her parents believed it was important for her to maintain her cultural identity as a Jew. She describes those summers, from ages eight to fifteen, as a fabulous experience. "The woman who ran the camp was named Hadassah Blocker. She introduced me, really, to spiritual life as a woman—to a deep and mystical appreciation of the Divine, as much as I could understand it as a small child."

We speak at length about these formative years at summer camp, and I am easily drawn into the magic and mystery of it all. I get a true sense of what it must have been like to be immersed in the old traditions, "the joy of the song and the dance and the old prayers." I can actually see Joan in my imagination, celebrating the Sabbath with her bunkmates.

Each week one girl in the camp was selected to be the Sabbath Queen and dressed in white. Six other little girls were dressed in blue to serve as her court. I am swept along by her narrative of a sacred ceremony in a pine grove and the innocence of young girls saying the ancient prayers, welcoming in the Sabbath as its brides.

It is easy to understand how these rich experiences molded Joan into being a lover of the mysterious. Combined with her innate curiosity as a child to understand the how and why of things, we can see how it was that she eventually became a scientist. Her entire life's journey has been a fascinating interweaving of intellect and soul—in high school, studying the world's religions and reading about the psychedelic experiences of Aldous Huxley; in college, exploring yoga and meditation; earning a degree from Harvard in medical sciences, becoming a cancer researcher, then teaching in the medical school at Tufts University and at Harvard. In the early 1980s, she co founded a Mind/Body clinic. "I have always been interested in consciousness, wanting to know, does consciousness lie in the brain? Is it in the body?" Many degrees and a body of recognized work later, it's not surprising that, today, "Dr. Joan" is considered to be one of the pioneers of mind/body science. Her relationship with and passion for a personal relationship with Spirit, remarkably, runs through it all.

I find myself intrigued by her thirst for scientific knowledge and how it has been so deftly interwoven into her quest for God. I learn from speaking with her that this integration has occurred because, time and again, she put herself full force into the murky stream of spiritual life—especially when there was doubt or decisions to be made. Joan perceived those questioning times not as something to be feared or avoided, but as unique opportunities to get to know herself better. To grow. To go, wherever she might be called. It is a process I describe as, "surrendering to our own unfolding."

This is our call as holy women, though it is not always an easy one to accept. Going with the divine flow of life as it is presents itself will not be without its problems or difficulties, as Joan attests. "They are inevitable as we grow. I certainly have had many of those," including two very difficult marriages, which she mentions, but does not elaborate on. "My own codependency, shall we say, has brought me to my knees."

She also refers to a lot of "mother-guilt" with raising two boys, especially through a long period of Sufi dancing—a spiritual trek through "a mystical Christian tradition, going to see various teachers, including Ram Dass and whatever Tibetan Buddhist was coming into town, while celebrating all the Jewish holidays." Over the years this resulted in "Waring-blender spirituality, composed of a little of this and a little of that." She chuckles at this now, and how other people have referred to her: "a Jewish, mystical Christian, Hindu, Buddhist, Native American psychoneuroimmunologist."[2]

I recall reading how she struggled during these searching years, unsure if honoring her "go-with-the-flow spiritual life" was the right thing to expose her children to. "I remember that time so well, Jan," she tells me. "I remember sitting around the kitchen table with my adult boys, the looks on their faces, as we talked about that time. My one son said, 'I really feel cheated in my Jewish heritage. I wish you'd sent me to Hebrew School. It's going to be hard for me to get it back now.' And then my other son saying, 'I'm so glad you didn't shove that down my throat. I only would have rebelled, and I'm so glad to be able to come to it in my own way.'" I can envision that scene at her kitchen table and wonder if I will ever have that same conversation with my own children. For they, like Joan's, have been raised with Waring-blender spirituality.

As we follow our heart and heed the whisperings of Spirit, we step out in blind faith. We say yes to the Spirit, even though we are unsure where our choices will lead. Or how they will ultimately affect the significant people in our lives, as Joan has experienced with her sons. We step out anyway, in trust. We trust that the Spirit, in the form of inner guidance, will serve as our compass as we traverse uncharted territory.

At the tender age of fifteen, Joan had her first experience of stepping out in trust. She was attending Girl's (Hebrew) School and being prepared for confirmation. "I remember very clearly sitting with the rabbi and experiencing a lot of stress. I'd begun to notice that women seemed to be marginalized in the Jewish religion. We're not part of a minion, which is ten men who gather to pray. I had really serious questions whether I wanted to take Judaism on as a spiritual path, because it didn't seem relevant to where women were in the world, and certainly not where I was as a young woman." She asked the rabbi about this and he offered her an explanation.

He told her that women are naturally spiritual—in their role of bearing life, raising children, keeping the home, and so on. "'You can't show up for prayer at a given point in time,' he said. 'You have more important things to do, which is why women in Judaism are excused from any prayer that's bound by time or place.'

And I thought right then, That's a kind of facile, silver-tongued devil explanation that I'm not having any of."

That experience sealed her fate for many years as a spiritual seeker outside the Jewish tradition. Starting in her teen years, Joan went on to explore many wisdom traditions, ultimately resulting in an eclectic spiritual bent. However, in 1998, at the age of fifty, something shifted inside her. She began to long for a spiritual connection with the Divine that was more focused, more personal. Her spiritual life had begun to feel dry. As she had done in the past whenever she felt this way, she went on pilgrimage. This time she went to India.

While there, she was graced with a myriad of experiences sourced in all the different religious traditions to which she had been exposed over the years. It was an intensely joyful and, at the same time, painful period of sifting and sorting, receiving and purging. On one of her final days there, she and her traveling companion, Andrea, went to a small synagogue. It was in that tiny place, built in 1568, that Joan finally reconnected with the Divine in an extraordinary way. A spontaneous urge to sing some life into the sad-feeling little synagogue took hold, and the two of them began to sing ancient Hebrew songs. Hearing herself singing in this way caused an emotional outpouring in Joan, accompanied by floods of tears.

It was only later that she realized what had been happening to her all throughout India, and especially in the synagogue: She was healing—letting go of all the bitterness and anger that had built up over the years as a result of woundedness caused by organized religion, teachers, and gurus she'd met along the way. Suddenly, "A peace that the Bible tries to describe as that which 'passeth understanding' enveloped me," she says.[3] It was the peace that comes from forgiveness. "No wonder my spiritual life felt dry," she wrote later in *A Woman's Journey to God*. "While I counsel other women to heal their religious wounds so that spirituality can find fertile soil to grow in a loving heart, my own wounds had been swept under the rug."[4]

In time, Joan revisited Judaism, adding more Jewish ritual into her personal practices. In doing so, she has come home to a very personal God, one who at times feels feminine, sometimes masculine, mostly a unique rendering of the two. "I decided that I could drink the Jewish Mystery without having to eat the box it was packaged in," she wrote. "Apparently you can take the woman out of the temple, but you can't take the temple out of the woman."[5]

Joan's pilgrimage to India was launched by a crisis of faith, though she did not recognize it as such at the time. By surrendering to her feelings, even though they were confusing, and heeding her spirit's urging to give in to her wanderlust for a bit, a powerful transformation was able to take place. This transformation is not so much about renewed faith as it is about being "more comfortable with less certainty and more mystery."[6]

What a potent invitation she offers us to surrender to the mysterious nature of our own journeys, to "let go and let God"! This is precisely what we must do. For women's journeys, by their very natures, *are* experiential and mysterious. Experiential, because we "feel" our way through them; with our bodily senses, heart, and mind we come to know the Divine in our own unique way. Mysterious, because there is truly no human way to decipher what is happening to us when we are in the midst of our own unfolding. Only in hindsight are we able to see how our experience has led us into the heart of the Holy One, that God was at work within us, guiding us through the circumstances in which we found ourselves. This is the Great Mystery made manifest. We don't understand how it works, but it always does, unfailingly.

Joan explains it this way: "We *can* trust life as it unfolds, whatever it is that it offers us. Even the scary things. They do take us where we need to go next . . . and we can trust that."[7] I imagine she might call those frightening things "blessings in disguise," as I do. Blessings in disguise are the bumps along the road of life that we experience. In the moment, they may feel horrible, but in time we will see that they imparted marvelous gifts.

My first significant blessing in disguise occurred when I was twenty-five. I was pregnant for the first time and overjoyed at the idea of becoming a mother. And yet, within weeks I knew something was very wrong. An ultrasound revealed no fetal heartbeat and the presence of a rare hormonal disorder. Almost four months into the pregnancy, my ecstasy died—along with my dreams of becoming a mother. I was devastated. As if that were not enough, the condition persisted in my post-pregnant condition. There was no way to make my hormones go back to their pre-pregnant state, except through one dramatic course of treatment—chemotherapy.

The next four months were the most hellish of my life. I will never forget the sensations of those times: loneliness paired with grief, hair loss and mouth ulcerations, and nausea and exhaustion beyond anything I'd ever experienced. And yet, I am amazed at the blessings that have continued to reveal themselves as a result of that difficult time.

These blessings are quite obvious to me today: gratitude for other babies when they came along, appreciation for good health, support from friends and family. Other blessings seem synchronistic and fated. Who would have known that years later I would conduct workshops and write books for women who were healing, especially from cancer? How else would I have been able to understand their feelings, as well as the effects of treatment, if I had not walked a similar path? When my father was diagnosed with cancer, I was able to accompany him through his dying with a deep understanding of how it feels to be lost in the bowels of fear. These blessings in disguise opened a doorway for me to step into the big questions of life—especially "Why?"—with faith and trust.

To live with Mystery in this way can actually be a form of spiritual practice in itself, say Frederic and Mary Ann Brussat, noted authors and founders of the popular website SpiritualityandPractice.com. "To be spiritual is to have an abiding respect for the great mysteries of life—the profound distinctiveness of other souls, the strange beauty of nature and the animal world, the ineffable complexity of our inner selves, the unfathomable depths of the inexplicable One."[8]

According to the Brussats, there are steps we can take to engage Mystery as a spiritual practice. The first is to cherish the baffling, the hidden, all the dimensions of our life that are inscrutable. "Give up that you can always get it," they say. "Be suspicious of all the 'ologies' that try to explain everything —from astrology to psychology to theology." The Brussats suggest that whenever we are

honestly stumped about anything, we should resist the
temptation even to ask "Why?" "Don't be afraid to admit
'I don't know.'"[9] Perhaps we can do as the Talmud, a
holy book of Judaism, suggests: "Accustom your tongue
to say, I do not know."

"I don't know" can actually become the practice.
Each time we utter these syllables, we surrender a little
bit more. We let go of our need to have everything tidy
and rational. We open ourselves up to grace because
we have created space within us for the Mystery to be
experienced in surprising new ways.

From this perspective, then, Mystery is not something
to be navigated, but something to be enjoyed, reveled
in, and appreciated, because it does inevitably take us
where we need to go—especially for our own healing
and wholeness. Not surprisingly, this seems to be where
Joan finds herself these days. "It is about understanding
the inner story," she says, "and flowing gracefully with
Spirit as it's moving in your situation." She refers to this
as "life artistry."[10] It is about being receptive to whatever
emerges.

In 2005, Joan, her husband, Dr. Gordon Dveirin, and
colleague Dr. Janet Quinn, founded a school for anyone
who desires to live into the questions more deeply. The
Claritas Institute for Interspiritual Inquiry is for spiritual
formation and learning the skill of mentoring others
within the world's wisdom traditions. Their book, *Your
Soul's Compass: What is Spiritual Guidance?*, is a wise
guide to being present to life as it unfolds, while, at the
same time, learning how to discern the Spirit's presence
in our lives.

This is what Joan, by her very essence, invites us to
do. To keep growing, keep listening, no matter where

our journey takes us. And how do we actually do this? By letting go of our own agenda and waiting patiently for the path to open step-by-step. We let go of the steering wheel of our lives and trust in a greater compassionate intelligence to guide us. "On the one hand," *Your Soul's Compass* explains, "surrendering to guidance involves the bone deep realization that we're helpless—no matter how hard we try to control things, we're ultimately *not* the sole author of our experience."[11]

As we are able to let go of control and let God in, we become increasingly aware that the "Other" that we thought was guiding us is not a separate One outside of ourselves at all. It is an indwelling Presence that has been with(in) us all along. We just needed to learn how to connect with it, to hear its voice and heed its wisdom. By doing so, we discover that we have actually cocreated an incredible life with divine assistance.

In the end, it is all about surrender to the Mystery— the ability to give ourselves over in trust to the journey, to know that everything that happens to us is in divine order, driven by divine purpose, for greater reasons beyond our immediate understanding. Surrendering in this way will bring us home to our truest self in God.

Joan Borysenko personifies for us the tenth Transformational Truth:

I Trust the Divine Timing
of My Own Unfolding

Joan told me once that she felt closest to God in nature. As a result, wherever her work has taken her, she has consistently chosen to live in the country, out in nature, rather than in the city. Considering that her father was a "nature mystic," and that Joan herself spent many years in the woods under the stars at summer camp, we can see the thread of that sacred connection running throughout her life.

Nature may be the most profound manifestation of the Divine in all its glory and mystery that any of us can encounter. Indeed, most of the mentors featured in this book can attest to that. Some of their earliest experiences of divine connection were experienced in nature

Perhaps it is because of its many paradoxes that this is so. Nature is powerful and gentle, unpredictable and seasonal, all at the same time. Its beauty is breathtaking, its force devastating. Depending on our experience of it in the moment, we may alternately savor it or fear it. Despite all our attempts to explain nature away by science and the "ologies," we cannot possibly understand it completely—or manipulate it. It invites us to live fully within its enigmatic presence. To be touched by it, awed by it. To serve it and steward it. To learn from it. Nature, like its Creator, invites us to live in its questions.

This is the image I hold of Joan, and the image I believe she would encourage each one of us to shape for ourselves: The nature lover, taking time each day to connect with the Presence as we experience it in nature, bending in closely to hear the whisperings of the Earth and its sacred secrets. The life scientist, ever inquiring, seeking to understand our world and how it works. Divine humans, we are a unique blend of inquiry and surrender, faith and reason—led by our intelligence, guided by the compass of our heart. Truly, we *can* learn to live and love the questions.

Perhaps poet Henry David Thoreau said it best: "My profession is to always be alert, to find God in nature, to know God's lurking places, to attend to all the oratorios and operas in nature." And, I would add, to attend to the oratorios and operas of our *own* lives. Indeed, doing so will reveal God in the midst of it all.

Reflection Questions

1. How well are you able to live with uncertainty, with not having all the answers? How does this create opportunities or problems for you in your day-to-day life?
2. In what ways have you experienced the mystery of the Divine at work in the events of your life? At work in nature?
3. What was one of your most powerful "blessings in disguise"? How did it impact your spiritual journey?

Peaceful Pause

Living with Uncertainty

Get into a comfortable seated position. Breathe deeply and evenly. Pay special attention to relaxing your face, neck, and shoulders. Place a slight smile upon your lips.

Gently place your hands in your lap, palms up, close together, to form a bowl. Now, bring to mind a particular issue that confuses you or seems beyond your understanding or control. Hold it clearly in your mind's eye, then allow it to drop down into your hands. Allow it to sit in this bowl of your hands.

Return your attention to your breath. Continue to breathe gently, with ease, allowing the confusing situation to rest peaceably in the bowl. Notice how it just sits there calmly, in comfort, in your hands.

Say to yourself:

> I allow any mental confusion or upsetting feelings I have to rest in this sacred holding. I release my need to strive to figure it out or to have an immediate solution. I trust that in time, clarity will come about this issue. I let go and let God make meaning of it when the time is right.

truth
eleven

I Courageously Speak and Live My Truths

Frances Moore Lappé

Something we were withholding made us weak
Until we found it was ourselves.

Robert Frost

Her wide, grinning smile naturally engages you. When she speaks, her voice is soft, refined, and inviting. It's hard to imagine that this woman, who has witnessed great suffering and vast injustice from Africa's plains to America's heartland, has an openness and vulnerability that can humble you as she speaks. You would think that one who has seen what she has would be hardened or cynical, yet activist Frances Moore Lappé has a heart as big as the world. Being with her makes you feel like crawling up inside her to be held by that enormous all-embracing heart of hers.

It was my daughter Taylor who "introduced" me to this woman who would help me finally conquer the disquieting fear I had about speaking my truths. You see, for most of my adult life, I'd lived my spiritual truths rather unobtrusively. My spiritual quest was kept close to my heart, a sacred secret between God and myself, as I tirelessly searched for him/her/it, the hallowed flavor of the day. Because I had resided for most of my adult life in a community with conservative religious ideals to which I did not subscribe, my spiritual search was done incognito. Only a few special friends knew of the spiral dance I was engaged in to find myself, eventually circling home to a spirituality of my own making. Writing this book is the final step in speaking the truth of who I have become—then publicly living that truth. Not surprisingly, as I made the commitment to do so, my ego kept rising to the surface, spitting epithets of fear and the woeful repercussions of truth-telling at me.

Enter my fear-releasing heroine. Taylor's middle-school class was taking a field trip to hear a guest speaker, an activist who had come to our community to promote a book she'd coauthored, *Hope's Edge: The Next Diet for a Small Planet*. My daughter left for school that day a typical, floundering-for-identity preteen; she returned full of zeal, transformed, certain her life's calling was to be an activist. "I want to be Frances Moore Lappé when I grow up," she said, and with that pronouncement, took immediate steps to live her life in harmony with Mother Earth as best a thirteen-year-old can. It involved recycling and consciously utilizing everything she could, including using a dishtowel for a napkin at meals (even taking one to school in her lunch box). She stopped shopping at the mall and bought her clothes at the Goodwill. She became a vegetarian who read every label and joined numerous environmental organizations, e-mailing legislators regularly. These "green" choices were not just a passing fancy for Taylor. As of this writing, it is now nearly five years since she encountered Frances, and she is as passionate as ever about a career devoted to environmental caretaking. I wondered, Who is this woman who helped my child fashion a new reality for herself within a matter of hours?

I should have known that the Universe would ultimately provide me with the opportunity to find out.

After Taylor's life-changing experience, it dawned on me that, as a magazine editor on the hunt for interesting news features, I had the perfect vehicle for connecting with this inspiring woman. I called Frances's office and arranged for an interview. I prepared for our conversation by reading her book *You Have the Power: Choosing Courage in a Culture of Fear* (coauthored with Jeffrey Perkins) and found it absolutely compelling. I researched her on the Web. She appeared to be the present-day version of Gandhi, "being the change" we all wished to see in the world. Frances has authored fifteen books and is a tireless global traveler, championing the causes of the world's hungry, our dwindling food supply, and the environment. As cofounder of the Small Planet Institute, she heads up a team of volunteers dedicated to bringing "living democracy" to communities on every continent. She is doing more single-handedly to heal our planet and its people than thousands of us put together. And she is doing it courageously, out loud, for all to hear, despite the fact that powerful people opposed her institute's findings or diminished their suggestions for change.

As our time together approaches, I am so in awe of her stature that nervousness prevails as I dial her telephone number. I take a deep breath and dive in, not wanting to waste a precious moment of this busy woman's time. I begin by asking her the question I always pose as I start these sorts of interviews: "Where is your heart right now as we begin our conversation?" I am greeted with silence. I can tell she is caught off guard by my question, so I wait.

"Truthfully," she offers slowly, "I am caught up in fear." More silence.

My anxiousness immediately abates as I attune myself to the vulnerability in her voice. "I'm sitting here at my desk," she says, "trying to write the sequel to my last book. This one's called *Democracy's Edge*. It invites citizens to come together to create the world they really want. I'm struggling with how to speak my truth. I see the world differently than I did a decade ago, and I want to make my views known, but not alienate people."

I can't believe what I am hearing. Here I was, bearing witness to a powerful woman whom I admire, as do millions of others—openly sharing her fear of expressing her truest self. What a powerful synchronicity!

Frankie, as she asks me to call her, continues. "If I'm listening to the message of my own book, the things that come up in me as I begin to write today are fear of failure, fear of not feeling like I can be true to myself, not being true to my own goals. Our social nature is our greatest gift and our greatest pitfall. We are so connected to one another, and we want to be true to the pack, yet we fear ostracism and are so vulnerable. This fear this morning has put my stomach in a knot, but that's okay, because I am at the edge of where I should be—struggling with exactly what I should be struggling with."

I am stunned that Frankie has given voice to exactly what I am struggling with, too. Here we are, both trying to pen books that reveal the truths we had come to know, and each of us is stuck, albeit temporarily, in the muck of fear. As she continues to share her process with me, by her own admission, she begins to feel better. "The first chapter of *You Have the Power* challenges us to see fear not as a verdict that we are on the wrong path, but, instead, as a signal that we are in the unknown, that we are taking a risk. By removing the judgment from it, that begins to free up the energy. Even talking to you about it right now, I feel my body relaxing a bit. Thank you for letting me speak about this."

To hear Frankie speak about the fear she feels, the fear we all experience when we are moving toward the unknown, opens up a portal of understanding for me. If someone like Frankie can openly confess to the fear that was paralyzing her, especially with someone she didn't even know, there is a message here for all of us.

Indeed, it strikes me that this is precisely what we must do. We must speak our truths, even if we're caught in the throes of gut-wrenching fear. The subtitle of Frankie's book says it all, naming the path every woman must take if she is to live as her most sacred self: *Choosing Courage in a Culture of Fear*. When we begin to have the awareness that, somehow, we can live in a new way, it is fear that rushes in to stop us before we even get started. It does not come in one guise, but many: fear of being different, fear of being ridiculed, fear of being judged, fear of being misunderstood. If we listen carefully to what is beneath these fears, a deeply embedded one emerges more clearly than the others: the fear of being cast out and left alone.

This is not the only fear that rises up. Fear of conflict looms large for women, as we are peacekeepers by nature. It is encoded in our DNA to bring people together, making sure that everything runs smoothly and everyone gets along. It's no surprise that "speaking one's truth" strikes terror in our hearts. If we speak what we know to be right and true for us, people may become angry, and the delicate balance of peaceability we strive for so deliberately may be tipped. And when it does, we're certain the resulting upset will have been all our fault.

When we begin to speak our truths publicly, fear naturally comes to call—fear of alienating our friends, family, coworkers, or neighbors. Such fear often relegates us to silence or to engaging in our spiritual journey unobtrusively or in secret. In a 2005 issue of *Breathe* magazine, actor and activist Susan Sarandon was asked by an interviewer why so many people are intimidated by the idea of speaking out, even becoming politically active. Her response, though tongue-in-cheek, rang true: "Well, look at what happened to poor Eve. The first person to think for herself, and she has the worst reputation of anyone. I mean, from the beginning of time we've been fed this notion that if you have knowledge, and you speak out, you'll be ostracized. So it's a very hard thing to take on."

As my conversation with Frankie continues, she reminds me of a powerful process she presents in *You Have the Power*: that we must continue to shift our "old thoughts" about fear like these into "new thoughts." Frankie and her coauthor, Jeffrey Perkins, consistently use this process themselves. Both writers openly share their own bouts with fear over the years and how they overcame them. For Frankie, the most recent episode occurred when she was diagnosed with breast cancer. For Jeffrey, it was when he openly admitted to the world that he is gay.

I find the process they used absolutely compelling, primarily because it is so darn practical! I gather from my conversation with Frankie that she is all about "practicality," simple actions that have the capacity to invoke positive change—and quickly. Brilliantly, she and Jeffrey hone in on seven classic thoughts we carry around inside of us, thoughts that keep us bound up in fear. Then they present seven corresponding new thoughts that allow us to break free of that fear.

Ironically, one of these "Old Thoughts" surfaces in the early minutes of our conversation. It is the first one presented in their book and, perhaps, the most crippling: "Fear means I'm in danger. Something's wrong. I must escape and seek safety."[1] Frankie advises, "When we feel it well up in our bellies, we think it means 'Stop.' What it really means is 'Go.'"

Hearing her speak of this stirs a memory of sage advice my father used to offer when I was younger and certain that the fear I was feeling was a sign for me to give up, no matter what the circumstance. "You must do the thing you think you cannot do," he would say. I discovered later that this thought was attributed to Eleanor Roosevelt. Her full remark, I found, was, "You gain strength, courage, and confidence by every experience in which you really stop to look fear in the face . . . Do the thing you think you cannot do."

I realize Frankie herself has just demonstrated perfectly how to disengage from fear when it comes to call—and how to not let it paralyze us. First, she acknowledged that the fear was there. She noticed what it was saying and how it was making her feel. She observed it, then spoke about it aloud to a listening, caring other—me. She watched how it tried to stop her. To observe our fear, as she did, means to watch it dispassionately, to keep an emotional distance from it—to witness it and not let it grab hold of us.

What do we do next? I wonder. Frankie answers, "The key is to *do* something. *Do* anything. Just *move!*

"When I'm feeling stuck I look at this picture on my wall of my friend and all-time hero, Wangari Maathai. Faced with personal, even physical attacks, and imprisonment for her pro-environment, pro-democracy work, she walked on. She has personally created a movement of village women planting trees throughout Kenya. It's called the Greenbelt Movement." I learn from Frankie that Kenya has experienced extreme deforestation. Twenty million newly planted trees later, Wangari's persistence and dedication have paid off. She is now the Deputy Minister of the Interior. In 2004, she became the first African woman to receive the Nobel Peace Prize—"for her contribution to sustainable development, democracy, and peace."

Frankie continues, "When I asked Wangari how she overcame her fears and frustrations, she told me, 'I just came home and started sweeping.' What that says to me is: Just move. Just do something. Sometimes that is all we can do, but when we do, things are set in motion. Once in motion, things begin to shift. Your perceptions shift. Things come to you that otherwise wouldn't come to you. This is one of the techniques I learned from Buddhist teacher Pema Chödrön. She says, just take a shower, go outside, just do something different! We don't have to be stuck.

"All the experiences I have gone through in life have taught me a lesson about myself: That I have this capacity to keep moving, and if I keep moving then new things happen, new energies enter in. I now know I can move with fear. It doesn't have to stop me."

Another fear that arises when we begin to speak publicly about what we believe is the fear of alienating our friends, family, colleagues, or neighbors. The "Old

Thought" is "If I'm really myself, I'll be excluded; if I break connection, I will be alone forever."[2] Making a new choice that honors our authentic self requires us to "choose our tribe," Frankie's book states. As we mature spiritually, we will experience change within our relationships. They are destined to change, in fact, because *we* have changed. It is also true that when we finally step out into the light of day as our truest selves, one of the risks we face is losing prized relationships.

"If we're willing to risk loss," *You Have the Power* says, "if we stand up, our actions declare that we have a vision of something the world needs. We then make it possible for others to *choose us*. When we stand up, we stand out. Think of it as sending a smoke signal, planting a flag, or lighting a beacon. . . . Only when we make ourselves visible do the right people for the right moment present themselves."[3] The "New Thought" we can embrace about speaking our truth is this: "To find genuine connection, we must risk disconnection. The new light we shine draws others toward us, and we become conscious choosers."[4] Support and companions do come. In the end, we are not alone, despite what we feared.

"If we feel we can't honestly move forward alone, we must ask ourselves who we know, who we can associate with, and who will help us believe in our forward energy," Frankie advises. "We can consciously draw toward us the people who will support us in that."

This is how we find a new community, a tribe, who accepts us as we are now. Frankie herself has experienced this again and again as she has taken a public stand on various issues. Some people were alienated by a particular stance she took, while new supporters stepped forward. Friendships and associations have waned in some areas and grown magnificently in others. Change, in this way, is a constant for the woman who stays faithful to her journey to wholeness.

I can't help but wonder what the source of this deep well of courage is that Frankie consistently draws from. How did she become so brave to live as she has? Was it because of her upbringing or a newfound spirituality? She alludes to Buddhism while we speak. Was it those teachings that helped her maneuver through entanglements of fear?

"My childhood was really quite extraordinary," she shares. "I was blessed to be unconditionally loved as a child. And if you haven't experienced that, it is hard to know what love looks like. My mother was the most loving person I've ever known."

There is silence from her end of the telephone, and I wonder where Frankie has gone. I wait. Within a few seconds, she haltingly begins again. Her voice is overflowing with emotion. "I'm sorry," she says. "That brought up so many feelings in me. I didn't expect that. I'm okay now."

My heart is tugged into a softer place knowing that this woman, considered by so many to be a pillar of strength, has the courage to be vulnerable, to share her naked emotion with me, a stranger. I'm even more curious now how this woman came to be the wonder that she is. Frankie continues, "My parents belonged to the Unitarian Church in the 1950s, during the McCarthy era, when membership in such organizations could result in accusations of Communism. It did for them. My parents were investigated. It was a painful time, yet they held true, especially my mother, to her passion for seeking the truth. It did not harden her. She was someone who could forgive anyone for something they had done."

Frankie's passion for truth-seeking is due, she believes, to her mother, who inquired into various spiritual philosophies her entire life. "She had a huge impact on me of being curious, of exploring the many different possibilities available to us in all areas of life. We're talking here about a simple housewife from Ft. Worth, Texas, who was asking the biggest questions of all including, how do we understand and make sense of our world?"

And because she was raised Unitarian, Frankie rarely heard the word "God": instead it was "Love," especially in the guise of community. "I was exposed to the spirituality of life and an energizing community of people who came together, often in our home, sitting at a cracked Formica kitchen table, conversation flowing well into the night." Within this church community, she had friends and attended youth gatherings and Unitarian camp, a rich experience for her. In her neighborhood and school it was a different story. "I was different, a Unitarian, and that was not a good thing. The girls my age literally cried for my soul. They were certain I would perish."

Today, Frankie describes herself as a "nightstand Buddhist." In the 1970s she read a book that had an enormous impact on her life: *Zen in English Literature* by R.H. Blythe. "I began to pick up other books on Buddhism (*Thoughts Without a Thinker* by Mark Epstein in the '90s and, in recent years, the work of Pema Chödrön) and discovered that all paths of Buddhism appealed to me. Tibetan Buddhism, though, is the one that rings most true." She tells me she does not belong to a formal community, or sangha, but "just a tight network of supportive friends."

The 1990s, Frankie explains, were very difficult for her, a period of great "disconnects," as she calls them. It was Buddhist teachings and the support of these friends who rallied around her that enabled her to move through what she describes as her "dark night of the soul." Loss and transition, divorce, moving to a new city, then in 2004, a diagnosis of breast cancer. "The Pema Chödrön teachings were very valuable to me at this time. I learned how profoundly humans are wounded. This deepened me. I learned to turn bitterness into compassion."

She speaks enigmatically about the emotional pain that remains. "The essence of what was so helpful to me from Buddhism in this difficult time was the notion of impermanence. Understanding that our suffering is in the grasping. Nothing stays the same. It always changes, even dies. This helped me live the life I've been given with so much change in it. I continue to push myself to get to the next unknown. Buddhism more than anything else has helped me live in the uncertainty of all of it. Everything changes. Everything is impermanent."

Frankie tells me she is still processing today why she made many of the life choices she did and how she is still learning from those choices. "I learned that I could deal with what had been handed to me," she says. "Life sometimes hands us our worst fears, but we can come out the other side. I did. Today I see all the experiences I have been given as a great gift."

In the weeks following my conversation with Frankie, I began to reframe my own relationship with fear. Instead of seeing the ego, the source of fear, as bad, I began to understand the important role it was playing in my spiritual journey. I noticed that each time a negative thought or feeling emerged, especially one about speaking and living my truth, I was being shown how I was still stuck in fear. It seemed that the ego's presence could illuminate the smallest areas within me where I was not free "to be me" and how I was still caught up in self-doubt or worry.

In Buddhist tradition, as Frankie so aptly modeled for me in our telephone conversation, there is a practice that can help one move through this more effectively. It is by being the Observer, the noticer of thoughts and feelings. In silence, or in meditation, we notice our thinking, label it as such, surrender those thoughts, then gently bring ourselves back to the present moment, back to our sacred center, where peace and love reside.

Let us remember that to have an ego is not a bad thing. In fact, the ego may be a profound gift of the Spirit, one that, properly observed, could be our greatest catalyst for spiritual growth. Granted, it does cause tension within us, as it did Frankie, but if we can observe our ego and its soul-freeing capabilities, we can then accept everything that happens to us throughout our lives as an opportunity for growth. Every incident, every encounter—good, bad, or indifferent—becomes spiritual fodder for our journey. Spiritual, because it requires us to choose Spirit over ego, the higher road over the lower, action over fear, time and time again. And when we do make that Spirit-filled choice to follow where the most authentic voice within us leads, an energetic shift takes place, and we begin to move away from what holds us back: from being bound as insecure, helpless humans toward living as powerful ones with divine roots and wings.

I am certain that Frankie had no idea when she shared her immobilizing fear with me that day how I would be fortified by her action to confront my own fear. Her honesty, her vulnerability, opened up a whole new world of possibility for me. I witnessed her notice the fear, then walk right through it. Frances Moore Lappé, without consciously knowing it, helped formulate the eleventh Transformational Truth:

I Courageously Speak and Live My Truths

Once we have embraced this truth, we must remember that any uncertainty, self-doubt, or fear that we may continue to experience is rooted only in our ego's need to be in control. The ego is sure it knows the best way for us to stay safe and secure. It doesn't like living in the unknown, but, alas, that is not the true nature of the spiritual journey. The quest to live our spiritual truths is ultimately shrouded in mystery. Buddhist teacher Pema Chödrön reminds us that "embarking on the spiritual journey is like getting into a very small boat and setting out on the ocean to search for unknown lands . . . sooner or later we will encounter fear. For all we know, when we get to the horizon, we are going to drop off the edge of the world."[5]

At this point in our journey, it takes great faith and trust to move toward a new version of ourselves because we are in uncharted waters; we have not been in this place before. Surely the way to arrive at the shores of spiritual well-being is to take one step, then another, into the unknown, and trust that the courage to proceed will come. In fact, Pema writes, "The next time you encounter fear, consider yourself lucky. This is where the courage comes in. Usually we think that brave people have no fear. The truth is that they are intimate with fear."[6]

This is what I have come to know to be true about Frankie. Her intimacy with fear and her ability to overcome its paralyzing effects have enabled her to become one of the most empowered women of our day. I read recently that the *Washington Post* deemed her one of the most visionary women of the twentieth century, along with Dorothy Day, Barbara Ward, Jeannette Rankin, and Margaret Mead. I feel so very blessed to have learned one of the most profound lessons of my life from her. I do my best each day to live up to the example she has set for me. Just as Frankie helped my daughter fashion a new reality for herself, she has helped me refashion my own.

Ever the luminary, Frankie continues to hold a powerful vision for all of us for the future. As of this writing, she has a new book out, *Getting a Grip: Clarity, Creativity, and Courage in a World Gone Mad*. It is possible, she claims, to quit grasping at straws and grab the real roots of today's crises, from hunger and poverty to climate change and terrorism. "My book's intent is to enable us to see what is happening all around us but is still invisible to most of us. It is about people in all walks of life who are penetrating the spiral of despair and reversing it with new ideas, ingenious innovation, and courage."[7]

Courage. There it is again, that potent virtue to which Frankie brings us back again and again. She never lets us forget how important it is for us to don the mantle of courage so we can speak and live our truths. The word "courage" comes from the Latin *cor*, meaning "heart." It denotes acts of bravery sourced in the heart. This is what

Frankie consistently models for us and desires for us, as well.

We *do* have a boundless future with unlimited possibilities ahead of us if we can become familiar with fear and rise above it through acts of courage. The deepest, truest part of us, our spirit, wants us to be all that we can be and desires us to move forward, to grow, to thrive; to live the divine freedoms latent within us—boundless joy, inner peace, and profound love for one another. If we cling to our fears, we cannot fly. As the Persian poet Rumi reminds us, "You were born with wings. Why prefer to crawl through life?"

And this is our choice each and every day—to discern which voice to listen to: the voice that takes us to our highest selves and most glorious future, or the voice that keeps us small, crouched in fear and impossibility. Let us listen well. Let us listen to our spirits and the whisperings of our hearts. "Only from the heart," says Rumi, "can you touch the sky."

Reflection Questions

1. What fears come up for you when you consider speaking your truth? Living as your truest self publicly?
2. What effect has fear had on your life? Have you used any specific techniques to successfully release yourself from these fears?
3. Do you consider yourself to be a courageous person? Why or why not? Reflect on a time when you experienced personal courage and how that incident may have changed your life.

Peaceful Pause

Transforming Fear

Close your eyes. Draw deeply upon your breath. Rest peacefully in the knowledge that any fear that may be present will begin to lessen its hold upon you with each breath you take. Inhale and exhale slowly, evenly, for as long as it takes to drop into your sacred center. Feel divine calm around you, moving through you, slowing your thoughts.

Gently become aware of any sensations of fear that linger inside of you. Imagine your palms, outstretched in front of you, ready to receive this fear. Allow any fear you've been feeling to come to rest in your hands. See it with your mind's eye and notice how small that fear really is—small enough to hold in your hands. How insignificant it looks just sitting there. *Notice that you are now holding your fear instead of it holding you.* Notice how much more peaceful you feel.

Continue to breathe easily, allowing the fear to simply be, and then, with each breath you take, watch it decrease in size. Observe it getting smaller and smaller with each breath until you can see it no more. Your fear is now gone. Breathe in a deep breath of freedom. Breathe out a prayer of gratitude for the divine breath that has moved through you, clearing out anything that holds you back from being your truest self in God.

truth
twelve

I Open My Heart to Others
and Celebrate Our Oneness

Mari Gayatri Stein

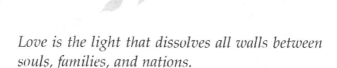

Love is the light that dissolves all walls between souls, families, and nations.

Paramahansa Yogananda

I did not know what I was in for when I stumbled upon her humorous drawings of dogs having enlightened conversations with humans. As editor, I was seeking a cartoonist for *Healing Garden Journal,* someone who could lend a bit of humor and wit to our life journeys. I found her within the pages of *Unleashing Your Inner Dog: Your Best Friend's Guide to Life.* Author/illustrator Mari Gayatri Stein, a yoga teacher from Oregon, soon became our resident artist of whimsy, offering a monthly column on the lighter side of spiritual life. Little did I know when I met her, what a powerful teacher she would become for me, opening my heart to a world of compassion and Oneness. But it all began with the dogs.

My first e-mails from her were hysterical. They were full of loving "woofs" and "wags." Everything she said was "light from the heart," encoded in doggie language. I learned Mari was a true "dog person," as they say (as opposed to some people being "cat people"), having an enormous love affair with border collies in particular. At one time she had six of them. She seemed to view her animal friends as wise spiritual teachers.

I soon realized that I was drawn to her work not so much for the dog wisdom, but for the love that was buried within it. She would send e-mails oozing with love and affection, which, truthfully, baffled me. She would address me as "dear heart" or "darling." We'd only connected through the airwaves. How was it possible for her to send so much love to someone she didn't even know? It was heartfelt love, too, not some phony, quasi-spiritual version of it. I could feel it course through me, like a wave of warmth whenever we connected. I was determined to know more about this intriguing woman whose words had such a powerful effect upon me.

Mari and I finally arranged to speak together in 2004 for the purposes of this book. To prepare, I'd immersed myself further in her life-affirming philosophies by reading another of her books, *The Buddha Smiles: A Collection of Dharmatoons*. From its contents, I assumed her to be Buddhist. Surely that would explain why she was so peace-filled and loving.

That is one of the first questions I ask her—Are you a Buddhist? Her response surprises me. "I don't call myself 'an anything' really, except a woman with faith, in awe of life's infinite possibilities. Ideas and labels are finite, and although they are invaluable as guidelines, they can be a real trap. I resonate with so many different belief systems and tenets of philosophy. Buddhism is a comfortable fit because of its principles of non-duality, spaciousness, inter-being, kindness in every breath, moment to moment mindfulness, spirit of openheartedness, and selfless service. I also feel drawn to various Hindu, Bhakti, and devotional practices— chanting and Karma Yoga. I love what Swami Sivananda said: 'Be good, do good, be compassionate; adapt, adjust, accommodate.'

"My grandparents were Russian Jewish immigrants, and I was born in Hollywood; I cultivate compassion for all cultures and endeavor to have a spacious and eclectic understanding of how people behave, make choices, and view life."

Spaciousness. It is a word that comes up again and again in our conversation. It is a concept that is of primary importance to Mari. Spaciousness is about being *open*—open to yourself, to life as it presents itself in the moment, and to those around you. Spaciousness is about living with a wide-open heart, welcoming and loving yourself as you are (even when you make mistakes); welcoming and loving others as they are, ego warts and all. Spaciousness, it seems, is the placeholder for love.

As Mari shares bits and pieces of her life story, I hear and feel spaciousness all around it. "I have dog-like traits," she admits. "I always err on the side of love. 'Better to be the one who smiled, than the one who didn't smile back,'" she quotes herself from *The Buddha Smiles*.

Like many people of her generation, she did a lot of experimenting in the 1960s, " . . . of seeking God in the sensual world of people, places, and things, where for a brief moment I could sense the infinite nature of a Divine Self, but it was not Self sustaining. Sex, drugs, rock and roll, and the reclamation of my soul," she quips. "I struggled with desire and aversion, with ambition and disappointment, with rapturous highs and demoralizing lows."

In her twenties, Mari longed for the answer, to find happiness, comfort and safety. She had moved through a career as an actress and a model into a career as a writer and an artist, but she often felt depressed and lost. "I really, really, wanted Spirit; I longed to press the veil, to know God. When I was in the throes of creativity—writing and drawing—I felt the connection, but it didn't last."

"Then my mother introduced me to yoga. I felt I had come home." As Mari explains, she's always learned best under fire, so she jumped right in. "I took my first teachers' training course and loved it. It was natural for me; I was transported. In the practice, I discovered a quiet place within me that didn't require anything but its own stillness. It was empty and full at the same time." That, she says, was her first sense of a power greater than herself that was tangible, but without form. At that time, she also realized that she couldn't control her use of intoxicants. "That was the next step and the first of twelve. I gave up altering my being with anything but Spirit. I chose sobriety and embraced a Higher Power. Actually, it was a grace. I felt God as an energy of pure love within and without, and in the company of kindred spirits, I embarked on a middle path of wholesome self-restraint and Self discovery. I let go." Mari tells me that her life was dramatically transformed from that moment on. She started to be of service to others, to teach, write, and draw inexhaustibly and to mentor those on a spiritual path. There was the sense of a daily miracle in her life that she could not explain.

"There was plenty of consistent footwork to do, but the inner freedom was a gift. Love flowed through me when I got out of my own way and surrendered to the joy of living one moment at a time."

I can't help but wonder about the spiritual teachings that contributed to this transformation, so I ask her. "The underlying current of my whole life has really been about two things: love and humor. It is about living with a love for oneself and others that is passionate and forgiving. A love that understands our human foibles and all our grasping, greediness, and clinging. Our denial, agitation, and doubts. Love suspends all that, accepts, and moves on." The essence of her teaching is this, Mari says: To come back to the present and begin again. No matter what has happened, no matter what behavior has lured us in, or what choice we have made, just address it and let it go. "We do this with compassion and understanding, with lovingkindness, with spaciousness, and of course, humor. 'Be kind' has become a mantra for me."

It's important for us, she says, to remember the big picture. "Remember, we're all in this together. We remember that it's nobody's fault. It's not about good and bad, right and wrong, because that is so unskillful and unproductive. The only thing that matters is that we begin again and try to learn something. We extend and open ourselves; we relate with openheartedness to someone who is suffering, because in that ignorance, we are all suffering. That's a fact. All we have to do is pick up a newspaper and read about what's going on in the world around us."

I am awed by her words. I think to myself, I don't know if I could ever be like that—be that open, forgiving, and nonjudgmental—about anything, about anyone. It feels to me as if this could take a lifetime to let go of my opinions and judgments; to move away from my self-certainty that I am right and everyone else is wrong. Indeed, it must take eons to learn to love everything and everyone that comes our way, as Mari seems to have done. This "openheartedness" feels, to me, like an onerous task. Yet because I trust the divine synchronicity of our meeting, I know that there is an opportunity here. Mari has opened a door for me, and on the other side I catch a glimpse of my true self—someone who does desire to be free from forming opinions and making judgments about others. I do want to be kinder, more openhearted, and more loving. But how?

I was given the opportunity to learn how almost immediately. I attended a seminar given by Elizabeth Liebert, PhD, a professor from San Francisco Theological Seminary. As I recall, she was speaking about practices we could use to center ourselves during our busy days. She suggested doing so at the computer while sending e-mail. We could take this opportunity to slow down, take a breath, and just be in the moment. I was intrigued by what she suggested.

Serendipitously, I had been struggling with my e-mail correspondence. Since getting to know Mari and receiving her love-imbued messages, I found myself stuck about how to sign off on mine. Mari always offered hugs or loving "woofs" and "wags." This gave me pause for reflection. Did she really feel that way about everyone she sent an e-mail to? Or was it just a chosen few? My guess was that she sent out a big wash of love to everyone. I found myself warming up to the idea that maybe, just maybe, I could try to do the same. I could shift from "sincerely" to something more loving. Perhaps doing so would even open up spaciousness in me. I was willing to give it a try.

Like Goldilocks testing the porridge, chairs, and beds of the Three Bears, I had to find the sign-off that fit me best. "All the best" was definitely too cold, "love" a bit too warm for a general farewell to just anyone, especially business associates. I landed on "blessings." "Blessings" felt just right. I chose it because it told the receiver exactly how I felt about them, which was, "You are special to me, and I wish you happiness." When I closed my e-mails with "Blessings, Jan," I imagined a glittery shower of good things falling lightly upon them.

I soon discovered it was easy to bless those I loved. It was much harder to confer a blessing of happiness or affection upon someone who I perceived to be gnarly or difficult, especially one who I believed had caused me hurt. For some unknown reason (grace, most likely), I refused to change the greeting to something more generic for prickly people. I vowed to stick with "blessings" and make it a spiritual practice. This is how it worked and still works for me today.

If I am not in a place of love and compassion for the person I am corresponding with by the end of the e-mail, I do not send it. It goes into the draft file. A response can go unsent for a number of hours (yes, sometimes days, if I am honest), until I am able to formulate a genuine, loving response and sign off with "blessings." In the period of time I have taken to respond, I've assessed my feelings for that person and determined if there is work to be done within me about this. I might pray or meditate. I allow time to pass to reveal how I might let go of any negative emotion that holds me captive. Then, when the time is right, when my heart feels open and loving, I send the e-mail. Spiritual Practice 101—that is what I call e-mail now.

In time, this practice has become easier for me. On most days, it is effortless to send e-mails off with love and blessings to just about anyone. If I am ever stuck, within a few seconds of recognizing my own gnarliness,

I can arrive at a place of equanimity. Thinking of Mari helps. I imagine her loving missives and take a few deep breaths. I use her as my role model for sending out a bouquet of e-mail love. The practice of blessing via e-mail has transformed me. It has opened my heart beyond my wildest imaginings.

As I am learning from Mari, openheartedness to others can only happen in proportion to how openhearted we are to ourselves. She speaks to me of gentleness, kindness, self-compassion. There is a pattern here, a strong and sturdy thread of truth that weaves through all our languaging and traditions. No matter whether we call ourselves Buddhist, Christian, Jewish, Sufi—or "nothing in particular, and at the same time everything," as Mari does—it is all the same. Our journey into the sacred begins with our relationship with ourselves and ripples out from there. What other practices can we do to keep our hearts open to others? None, until our own hearts are open to what lies within them. *Metta*, from the Buddhist tradition, is one such practice for the purpose of cultivating lovingkindness for ourselves and others. We begin by directing metta—lovingkindness—to ourselves first.

Sitting quietly, we can mentally repeat, slowly and steadily, the following or similar phrases: "May I be happy. May I be well. May I be safe. May I be peaceful and at ease."[1] Lovingkindness meditation consists primarily of connecting to the intention of wishing ourselves and others happiness. After a period of directing lovingkindness toward ourselves, we then bring to mind a dear one, someone in our life for whom we care deeply. We slowly repeat phrases of lovingkindness toward them: "May you be happy. May you be well. May you be safe.

May you be peaceful and at ease." In time, we will find ourselves able to send our lovingkindness to others— friends, neutral others, difficult others, even enemies. Finally, we direct lovingkindness to every single human being on earth. Buddhist teacher Sharon Salzberg tells us that this practice proceeds in a very structured way. Through repetition, with time and grace, "We open up our limits and extend our capacity for benevolence," she says. "Through the power of this practice, we cultivate an equality of loving feeling toward ourselves and all beings."[2]

What I also appreciate about Mari is her unique ability to take spiritual practice and enliven it with humor. Her penned "Dharmatoons" have often brought me back to center as I witness the seekers in her book—both human and animal—struggle with their own lovingkindness and ability to stay openhearted. "On the whole, everything has its little thorns, and that's what I draw about. Especially forgiveness, because that is what frees us. That's what allows us to relax and smile and say, 'Oops, did I say that? Did I think that?'"

Though yoga and Buddhist teachings have been at the core of her life philosophies for a very long time, faithful student that she is, Mari remains alert to however the teacher may come, no matter the spiritual tradition. "I think the essence of all spirituality is the same," she says, "and that's what interests me—the essence. I'm completely open to anything happening. It's like having a vast buffet. You can fill your plate with all of it, or just take what you want and leave the rest. Just be true, be authentic."

Knowing this, I should not be surprised to learn that she has been deeply influenced by a woman of a very different spiritual persuasion from her own—Mother Teresa of Calcutta. In fact, Mari and her husband, Robert, had the opportunity to actually meet her in India in the 1980s. Delighted to hear this, I beg her to tell me the story. I cannot imagine what it might have been like to actually meet her, this woman deemed by a Gallup Poll as the most respected and admired person of the twentieth century. Mari tells me how they set off to India with a group led by an Indian teacher named Sant Vadas Keshavadas, known as 'the singing saint.' "The trip was full of singing, chanting, and merriment, and an all-pervading feeling of Spirit." She and Robert left the tour at one point and went on to Kashmir, eventually visiting one of Mother Teresa's orphanages for homeless children in Calcutta.

"There we were on a sweltering afternoon, the heat and fatigue dampening our eagerness. And then, there she was. Mother Teresa appeared invincible. She had the one-pointed focus of a border collie but none of the cuddliness. I couldn't take my eyes off her. We were spellbound by her energy. There was nothing airy-fairy or other worldly about her. She was compelling—bare bones authentic. She inspired confidence and made you feel that you too could be a transforming force in the universe. This diminutive woman, in her white sari and headdress trimmed in cornflower blue, was a power-house. She was a strong little whirlwind of a woman, just whoosh, whoosh, whoosh—no time squandered on amenities. Her words and actions said, 'Don't waste time. We're on a mission here. If you want to be helpful, get busy now.'

"So we all hurried to keep pace with this energetic and seemingly ageless, but aged, petite, wiry woman. When asked by a man in our group what we could do to help, her answer was succinct and brusque, but impersonal. No time for hurt feelings and niceties. She turned to us and said in her commanding and heavily accented voice, 'Look to those around you, to your family, your neighbors and friends. Do they need help? Are they hungry? Are they lonely? Can you offer them comfort?'

"Before we could catch our collective breath, she had brought us down to what matters." Mari explains how she interpreted Mother Teresa's questions. "To me she was saying: 'What are you doing over here looking for enlightenment? Living with love is your Dharma. You don't need to travel around the world to be of service. Open your eyes to those around you. Be helpful and be loving. Share what you have, give of yourself. Offer succor to others; begin in your own home, in your own family, on your own block, in your own soul.'

"It was inspiring, exhilarating, and in its simplicity, somewhat of an embarrassment. Basically, she told us to go back home and attend to the people in need around us. That was not what we expected to hear." Mari was forever changed by her Indian experience and her encounter with Mother Teresa, though not in ways she'd envisioned when her journey began. It caused her to reevaluate how hospitable she was to others, how generous of time and spirit she was. How open her mind and heart were to the needs of those around her.

I have thought of Mari's Mother Teresa story often since she shared it with me. I reflect upon the powerful invitation that was offered to her, to all of us, and I am humbled by it time and again. Like Mari, it brings me back to what matters, with questions such as:

Am I being loving today?

Is my heart open to others?
Am I welcoming to others, even
    strangers?
Am I sympathetic to the plight of my
    fellow human beings?
Am I doing something to lend
    assistance?

What I find most compelling about Mari's story is that
Mother Teresa did not just tell her visitors to go home
and do good works. Mother directs all of us to look
inward—to look at the condition of our own soul—and
to take care of that. As Pema Chödrön would say, "You
work on yourself in order to be able to work with other
people." And as we are able to do so, we will deepen in
self-love and self-compassion. In time, this love will flow
freely out toward others. By its very nature, it cannot
help but do otherwise. Working on ourselves is work for
the betterment of humanity.

How we perceive ourselves in relation to others is
key to living in a sacred manner. As Mari tells me, if we
hold fast to our opinions and judgments of others, we
continue to keep ourselves closed off from one another.
My opinions about you, and yours about me, keep us
separated. And yet, if I am a divinely sourced being, and
you are, too, aren't we the same? Aren't we all walking
a sacred path, hoping to unite with the Source? Aren't
we all praying for connection, hoping for relief from the
suffering and pain life brings? Becoming aware of pain
and suffering, our own and that of others, can actually
bring us closer to one another.

Since her open heart surgery on the eve of the new mil-
lennium, Mari tells me that she loses approximately one
week a month to illness, to pain, "to some preoccupation

with my body that needs to be attended to. Whether it's going to the doctor, or not doing everything I wish I could do, that in itself has to be a spiritual practice, because nothing is outside of practice." She says, "There is no 'if only. . . .' 'If I could get this part of my life right, everything would be fine.' No, this is it."

The reality of life is that we all have pain of some sort—physical, emotional, spiritual. We all suffer. "The practice is to be present with every other human soul and wish that none of us would have to suffer," she says. "As a child, I was empathetic. I knew there was suffering everywhere, and there was a part of me that knew I couldn't be free until all people were free." What she is referring to here is known in Buddhist tradition as the Way of the Bodhisattva: A being who is so awake, so aware of the nature of the world, of humanity's plight and the suffering of others, that they put off their own enlightenment until "all sentient beings are free from suffering." In previous chapters such beings were referred to as angels. They remind us that we, too, can be angels to one another. To act as a Bodhisattva or "earth angel," one who reaches out with hands and heart to assist others, is a possibility for each of us. In fact, it may be what we are born to do.

Through developing awareness of our suffering— how we get trapped in the confines of our own ego—we can begin to be of service to one another. We can remain mindful that we are *all* walking this thorny path. We are *all* asking ourselves, "How can I be more free?" Being aware of our ego entanglements gives birth to compassion for others who are struggling, suffering, just as we are. In that similar cause, we are one.

We are a myriad of ones all seeking the One. We are all holy women and men seeking our peace, our joy, our eternal happiness. You and I are no different, no different at all. We are one body in many bodies, all trying to get "home" to the larger body—God—that encompasses us all.

This final leg of our journey as divine human beings is about awakening to our Oneness. Thomas Merton put it this way: "The deepest level of communication is not communication, but communion. It is wordless. It is beyond words, and it is beyond speech, and it is beyond concept. Not that we discover a new unity. We discover an older unity. My, dear, we are already one. But we imagine that we are not. And what we have to recover is our original unity. What we have is what we are."[3]

I believe that we *will* recover this original unity when we are able to truly bless one another. This is what Mari does throughout her day and she invites us to join her. By blessing, or sending metta, we will no longer regard ourselves as different and separate from one another. We will perceive each human being, each soul, as an extension of ourselves, and in that glorious moment when we can, we will, usher in a reality of Oneness.

With Mari Gayatri Stein as our guide, we can realize the twelfth Transformational Truth:

I Open My Heart to Others and Celebrate Our Oneness

It has been more than four years since I began it, but I have remained faithful to my spiritual e-mail practice. I'm still signing off with that powerful word of benediction—"blessings." It is my way of saying "namasté," a salutation I learned in my first yoga class in the '70s. As I understand it, the term namasté was a greeting used by Hindustani pilgrims as they hiked through the Himalayas. As their paths crossed, they would stop, bow, and say "namasté" to one another, a salutation of honor and respect for that person and his or her journey. *"The Spirit in me meets the same Spirit in you."* Whether it is "namasté" or "blessings", it reminds me, we are one.

Each morning when I go to my computer I am met with a statement by Mother Teresa, one I purposefully placed upon the monitor after meeting Mari. It reads, "Let no one ever come to you without leaving better and happier. Be the living expression of God's kindness: kindness in your face, kindness in your eyes, kindness in your smile." This quote, read daily, keeps me attuned to the invitation to perpetually love others as best I can.

This has been my experience of Mari: absolute kindness, unconditional love and compassion, true humility. She is, in her own way, in her small corner of the world, doing the work of the Bodhisattva. She is blessing the world, one person at a time, in the hopes that someday we will all be free from suffering. I bow to her for that, and for opening me up to the unlimited possibilities of my own lovingkindness.

As our "official" interview for this book comes to a close, I ask Mari for a final word, a pearl of wisdom, to sustain us on our pilgrimage. "Love and laugh," she says without hesitation, offering the same two jewels with which she began our conversation. "And, take pleasure in the moment.

"Be kind."

Reflection Questions

1. Do you take time each day to assess how loving and openhearted toward others you are? Do you ever send loving thoughts or prayers to others?
2. In what ways do you demonstrate lovingkindness on a daily basis? Kindness to yourself? Kindness to others?
3. Have you ever had an experience of unitive oneness? If so, how did it change your spiritual life? Your day-to-day interactions with others?

Peaceful Pause

Openheartedness

Stand, stretching tall, arms out to the sides. Connect with your breath. Feel its calming presence wash through you. Bend slightly backward, arching your heart upward. Breathe. Focus your attention on your heart center. Lift it toward the sky.

Visualize your heart opening, widening, allowing love to flow in. Open yourself to others, to everything that lives and breathes on the earth, to the Divine One itself. Holding that position, offer the following prayer, silently or aloud:

> I desire to live in an openhearted manner. I ask that your love move through the vessels of my heart and clear out anything that keeps me from being my truest, most loving self. May my heart remain open to all who cross my path, even if they appear to be different from me. May my heart remain open to all living things. May I always remember that we are all creations of the Divine One who is the source of everything.

Epilogue

The bud
stands for all things,
even for those things that don't flower,
for everything flowers, from within,
    of self-blessing;
though sometimes it is necessary
to reteach a thing its loveliness,
to put a hand on the brow
of the flower,
and retell it in words and in touch,
it is lovely
until it flowers again from within,
    of self-blessing.

Galway Kinnell

American poet Galway Kinnell, like many a wise teacher, gives voice to what often remains unsaid, but is housed deep within us. In these few precious words, he captured my heartfelt desire for all who are awakening to their truest selves: that we will come to remember our innate loveliness; that we will begin to see ourselves as truly beautiful in body, mind, and spirit; that we will embrace ourselves as the sacred—holy and whole—women we are meant to be.

My intention when I began this writing was to put words upon the page that would serve as the gentle hand to the brow that Kinnell describes. Hope prevailed that my well-placed hand, along with the hands of the guiding women who have graced these pages, would cradle

243

your cheeks, lay softly upon your shoulders, holding you in warm embrace as we whisper, "Remember your loveliness. Remember who you are."

And with those words, you would rise, we would all rise, and spread the word of our glory to all the women who have not yet heard the message; to the women who are still bent low, unable to see the beauty of their own essence; to the women who are just beginning to look upward, but stumbling along the way. My hope today is that as each one of us remembers our true essence and begins to live from that pinnacle of empowerment, we will pause on our pilgrimage and take note of who is there behind us in need of a helping hand and humbly offer our own. And as we do, we will look deeply into each woman's eyes and offer her a silent blessing of love, of courage, of hope for the journey ahead.

Blessing. What a powerful word! Until recently, I had considered blessing a loving act I could bestow upon others. Reading Kinnell's poem and the writings of Buddhist teachers Sharon Salzberg and Sylvia Boorstein in the final days of this writing have caused a shift within me. My spiritual life has taken yet another turn in the road, this one an Eastern fork, because this practice of metta—sending lovingkindness—is transforming myself and my spiritual life. I see with renewed clarity how very important it is for us, especially as women, to bless ourselves by tenderly laying our own hand upon our own brow and wishing ourselves well. For in that self-loving gesture, we will engage in deeper healing and, as a result, we, too, will blossom. By self-blessing we retell ourselves, in words and in touch, "I am lovable . . . I am loving . . . I am lovely . . ."

We will embark on pilgrimage again and again as we seek to embody our truest selves more and more each day. May I humbly offer a traveler's blessing for our journey. In the spirit of metta, I bestow a blessing upon myself first, then upon you, then upon all women who are awakening, and even upon those who are not yet aware of their divine nature. This blessing is sourced in the twelve Transformational Truths.

A Blessing for Embodying Your Truest Self

May I remember my sacred identity. May I feel holy and whole.

May I honor the calling of my spirit and follow its guidance as I create a rich spiritual life for myself.

May I listen respectfully to the whispers of my body and trust that it will serve me well as a conduit of sacred wisdom.

May I cultivate thoughts, feelings, and practices that enable me to live as the peaceful, joyous, loving being I naturally am.

May I love and care for myself on a day-to-day basis as tenderly as I care for others.

May my eyes be open to perceive, my heart open to receive the divine presence in each person who crosses my path.

May I remember that I am divinely guided, loved, and supported in every moment, in all that I do.

May I know that when difficulties arise, I am being invited to let go of something that no longer serves my truest self.

May I have the strength to make positive new choices for myself each and every day to live my highest purpose.

May I have the courage to live with uncertainty and overcome my fears so I can live as the vibrant woman I am meant to be.

May I demonstrate unconditional love and compassion for others. May my efforts contribute to the creation of a new world community, rooted in peace and love.

As you bless yourself with these words, know that you are a vital part of a grand and glorious community of women, all of whom are blessing themselves and one another. Together, we are transforming ourselves, and transforming the planet, one blessing at a time.

May you remember your loveliness. . . .

Blessings,
Janice Lynne Lundy
February 2008

Notes

My True Identity Is Spirit

1. Brian Hunt, introductory text in blank journal (San Francisco: Chronicle Books, 1999).
2. Thomas Keating, *Intimacy with God: An Introduction to Centering Prayer* (New York: Crossroad Publishing Co., 2002), 163.
3. Ibid., 163.
4. Karen Casey, *Daily Meditations for Practicing the Course* (New York: HarperCollins Publishers, Inc., 1995), 63.
5. Joan Chittister, O.S.B., *Called to Question: A Spiritual Memoir* (Lanham, MD: Sheed & Ward, 2004), 13.
6. Megan Don, *Falling into the Arms of God: Meditations with Teresa of Avila* (Novato, CA: New World Library, 2005), 3.

I Am Free to Live a Spiritual Life of My Own Making

1. Joyce Rupp, *Dear Heart, Come Home: The Path to Midlife Spirituality* (New York: Crossroad Publishing Co., 1997), 55.
2. Phil Cousineau, *Pilgrimage: Adventures of the Spirit*, edited by Sean O'Reilly and James O'Reilly (San Francisco: Traveler's Tales, Inc., 2000), xv.
3. Carol Lee Flinders, *At the Root of This Longing: Reconciling a Spiritual Hunger and a Feminist Thirst* (San Francisco: Harper-SanFrancisco, 1998), 168.
4. Joan Chittister, O.S.B., *Called to Question: A Spiritual Memoir* (Lanham, MD: Sheed & Ward, 2004), 21.
5. Marion Woodman, as referenced by Sue Patton Thoele, *Heart Centered Marriage: Fulfilling Our Natural Desire for Sacred Partnership* (Berkeley, CA: Conari Press, 1996), 21.
6. Joyce Rupp, *Prayers to Sophia* (Notre Dame, IN: Sorin Books, 2000), 16.
7. Ibid., 16.
8. Joyce Rupp, *Walk in a Relaxed Manner: Life Lessons from the Camino* (Maryknoll, NY: Orbis Books, 2005), 56.
9. Ibid., 40.

I Trust My Body's Divine Connection

1. Jan Phillips, *Divining the Body: Reclaiming the Holiness of Your Physical Self* (Woodstock, VT: Skylight Paths, 2005), 96.
2. Jay Michaelson, *God in Your Body: Kabbalah, Mindfulness, and Embodied Spiritual Practice* (Woodstock, VT: Jewish Lights, 2007), ix.
3. Jan Phillips, *Divining the Body*, x–xi.
4. Jan Phillips, *Marry Your Muse: Making a Lasting Commitment to Your Creativity* (Wheaton, IL: Quest Books, 1997), 3.
5. Sue Monk Kidd, *The Dance of the Dissident Daughter: A Woman's Journey from Christian Tradition to the Sacred Feminine* (New York: HarperSanFrancisco, 2002), 23.
6. Joanna Laufer and Kenneth S. Lewis, *Inspired: The Breath of God* (New York: Doubleday, 1998), 19.
7. Jan Phillips, *God Is at Eye Level: Photography as a Healing Art* (Wheaton, IL: Quest Books, 2000), 7.
8. Phillips, *Divining the Body*, 19.

I Choose Thoughts and Feelings
That Honor My Sacred Self

1. Dorothy Hulst, *As A Woman Thinketh* (Marina Del Ray, CA: DeVorss & Co. Publishers, 1982), 4.
2. Ibid, 6.
3. Pema Chödrön, *The Places That Scare You: A Guide to Fearlessness in Difficult Times* (Boston, MA: Shambhala, 2002), 27.
4. Hulst, *As A Woman Thinketh*, 10–11.
5. "Interview with Jon Kabat-Zinn," *Body + Soul*, June 2005.
6. Thomas Keating, *Intimacy with God: An Introduction to Centering Prayer* (New York: Crossroad Publishing Co., 2002), 81.

I Engage in Daily Practices That Nurture My Spirit

1. Alen MacWeeney and Caro Ness, *Spaces for Silence* (Boston, MA: Tuttle Publishing, 2002), 36.
2. Wayne Teasdale, *The Mystic Heart: Discovering a Universal Spirituality in the World's Religions* (Novato, CA: New World Library, 2001), 1–2.
3. Ibid., 86.

I Cultivate Compassion for Myself

1. Sue Patton Thoele, *The Courage to Be Yourself: A Woman's Guide to Emotional Strength and Self Esteem* (Berkeley, CA: Conari Press, 2001), 113.
2. Sue Patton Thoele, as referenced by Jan Forrest, *Coming Home to Ourselves: A Woman's Journey to Wholeness* (West Olive, MI: Heart to Heart Press, 1999), 81.
3. *American Heritage Dictionary of the English Language* (Boston, MA: Houghton Mifflin Company, 1980), 272.
4. Joan Borysenko, PhD, and Miroslav Borysenko, PhD, *Inner Radiance: Weekly Engagement Calendar* (Carlsbad, CA: Hay House, 1995).
5. Sue Patton Thoele, *The Courage to Be Yourself*, 191.
6. Anne Morrow Lindbergh, *Gift from the Sea* (New York: Pantheon Books, 1983), 58–59.
7. Wayne Muller, *Sabbath: Finding Rest, Renewal, and Delight In Our Busy Lives* (New York: Bantam Books, 1999), 5.
8. Sue Patton Thoele, *The Woman's Book of Soul* (Boston, MA: Conari Press, 2000), 175.
9. Sue Patton Thoele, *The Mindful Woman: Gentle Practices for Restoring Calm, Finding Balance, and Opening Your Heart* (Oakland, CA: New Harbinger Publications, 2008), 2.
10. Ibid., 44.

I Experience the Divine in Everything and Everyone

1. Daphne Rose Kingma, *Loving Yourself: Four Steps to a Happier You* (Boston, MA: Conari Press, 2004), 6.
2. Daphne Rose Kingma, *The Future of Love: The Power of the Soul in Intimate Relationships* (New York: Doubleday, 1998), 25.
3. Kingma, *Loving Yourself*, 147.

I Know Divine Assistance Is Available to Me at All Times

1. Doreen Virtue, *How to Hear Your Angels* (Carlsbad, CA: Hay House, 2007), 1.
2. Ibid., 1.
3. Ibid., 3.

4. Carol Lee Flinders, *Enduring Grace: Living Portraits of Seven Women Mystics* (New York: HarperCollins Publishers, 1993), 84.
5. Doreen Virtue, *Messages from Your Angels: What Your Angels Want You to Know* (Carlsbad, CA: Hay House, 2002), 157.
6. Virtue, *How to Hear Your Angels*, 47.
7. Ibid., 48–50.
8. Doreen Virtue, *Healing Words from the Angels: 365 Daily Messages* (Carlsbad, CA: Hay House, 2007), 32.
9. Antoinette Sampson, *Peace Angels* (New York: Warner Books, 2001).

I Acknowledge That Difficult Times Bring Healing and Deeper Wisdom

1. Naomi Judd, *Naomi's Breakthrough Guide: 20 Choices to Transform Your Life* (New York: Simon & Schuster, 2004), 6.
2. Ibid., 36.
3. Thomas Merton, *A Book of Hours*, edited by Kathleen Deignan (Notre Dame, IN: Sorin Books, 2007), 122.
4. From the foreword of this book, xi.
5. Mirabai Starr, *Dark Night of the Soul: Saint John of the Cross* (New York: Riverhead Books, 2002), 11.
6. Ram Dass, *Still Here: Embracing Aging, Changing, and Dying* (New York: Riverhead Books, 2000), 129.

I Can Create My Life Anew Each Day

1. Gerald May, *Addiction and Grace: Love and Spirituality in the Healing of Addictions* (San Francisco: HarperSanFrancisco, 1988), 14.
2. Ibid., 14.
3. Ibid., 16.
4. Julia Cameron, *The Artist's Way: A Spiritual Path to Higher Creativity* (New York: Tarcher/Putnam, 1992), 3.
5. Matthew Fox, *Creativity: Where the Divine and the Human Meet* (New York: Tarcher/Putnam, 2002), 5.
6. Ibid., 18.
7. Michelle Tsosie Sisneros, "The Long Walk," 2004 (This is a poem on the back of one of her greeting cards).

I Trust the Divine Timing of My Own Unfolding

1. Rainer Maria Rilke, *Letters to a Young Poet* (Novato, CA: New World Library, 2000), 35.
2. Joan Borysenko, PhD, *A Woman's Journey to God* (New York: Riverhead Books, 1999) 16.
3. Ibid., 42.
4. Ibid., 40.
5. Ibid., 41.
6. Ibid., 43.
7. www.joanborysenko.com
8. www.spiritualityandpractice.com
9. Ibid.
10. Joan Borysenko, PhD, and Gordon Dveirin, EdD, *Your Soul's Compass: What is Spiritual Guidance?* (Carlsbad, CA: Hay House, 2007), 17.
11. Ibid., 6.

I Courageously Speak and Live My Truths

1. Frances Moore Lappé and Jeffrey Perkins, *You Have the Power: Choosing Courage in a Culture of Fear* (New York: Tarcher, 2004), 41.
2. Ibid., 149.
3. Ibid., 136.
4. Ibid., 149.
5. Pema Chödrön, *When Things Fall Apart: Heart Advice for Difficult Times* (Boston, MA: Shambhala, 1997), 1.
6. Ibid., 5.
7. www.gettingagrip.net

I Open My Heart to Others and Celebrate Our Oneness

1. "Facets of Metta," Sharon Salzberg, www.vipassana.com.
2. Ibid.
3. Thomas Merton, *A Book of Hours,* edited by Kathleen Deignan (Notre Dame, IN: Sorin Books, 2007), 162.

Acknowledgments

My heart overflows with gratitude for God, the Spirit, around and within. And for Mother Mary. Her guiding presence was felt through all the stages of this work, especially in leading me to the doors of Ave Maria Press, Inc.

Heartfelt thanks to Joyce Rupp, a woman of grace and generosity, for opening those doors. To Publisher, Tom Grady, and Editorial Director, Bob Hamma, for welcoming me and for seeing the potential of this book. To Susana Kelly, for her gentle editing skills and for her lightness of being. To everyone at Ave Maria Press, Inc. who had a guiding hand in this project, thank you for your soulful contributions. I feel blessed to be working with such Spirit-filled people.

Gratitude and glory to each of the twelve women featured within these pages for opening their hearts and sharing their lives with me, with all of us. I am humbled by your transparency, vulnerability, and passion for serving the Spirit and humanity. I wouldn't be the woman I am today without having journeyed with you, and for that I am so very grateful.

Love and gratitude to three of these women, in particular, for their lasting and profound influence on my life. Sue Patton Thoele, Daphne Rose Kingma, and Mari Gayatri Stein, mentors for life, for being perfectly human models of divine compassion. I carry you in my heart wherever I go.

Boundless appreciation to Pam Daugavietis, Jan Francisco, and Claire Gerus who gently critiqued the early stages of this manuscript and waved me onward.

Special thanks to the sisters, associates, and staff of Dominican Center at Marywood for hospitality, spiritual formation, and sacred space to continue to grow in the Spirit. Your unconditional, spiritual friendship is a grace.

To *Women's LifeStyle* and its publisher, Victoria Upton, who continues to give me the rare gift of being able to express my truest self in writing each month.

Big Love to my family for their unwavering affection and support, especially my parents, Jim and Lorraine Deremo, and my children, Casey, Kyle, and Taylor. You are my treasures.

Finally, this book would not have been birthed, nor would my truest self, if it had not been for my beloved husband Brad—the ultimate creative partner, spiritual companion, and lover of my soul. You did good, honey; the goddess is home.

About the Spiritual Mentors

Joan Borysenko, PhD, is a Harvard-trained medical scientist and licensed psychologist. A pioneer in psychoneuroimmunology and behavioral medicine, she is the founding member of Mind/Body Health Sciences, LLC, and director of the Claritas Interspiritual Mentor Training Program. She is the author of fourteen books, including *Your Soul's Compass: What is Spiritual Guidance?* To learn more about Joan, visit her website: www.joanborysenko.com.

Dudley Evenson is a multimedia producer, photographer, harpist, and cofounder of independent record label Soundings of the Planet. She and her husband, Dean Evenson, have produced more than fifty albums since founding Soundings in 1979. They travel worldwide, teaching workshops on sound healing and other themes, and are producing a DVD about sound healing. They have three children and one grandchild. Their upcoming autobiography is called *Living the Dream.* You can learn more about Dudley by visiting her website: www.soundings.com.

Naomi Judd is a passionate communicator, whether she is singing, writing, speaking, or hosting her weekly television show, *Naomi's New Morning,* on the Hallmark Channel. Through a recovery from potentially fatal hepatitis C she has become a vocal proponent of Mind/Body medicine and women's healing journeys. Her most recent book is *Naomi's Guide to Aging Gratefully.* To learn more about Naomi, visit her website: www.naomijudd.com.

Daphne Rose Kingma is the author of eleven best-selling books about love and relationships, including *Coming Apart, True Love, The Men We Never Knew,* and *The Future of Love.* An international speaker, teacher, and workshop leader, she has been a six-time guest on *Oprah* and for more than twenty-five years was a psychotherapist and a teacher of relationships as a spiritual art form. She is now writing poetry and fiction, which she performs in Satsang Salons throughout the world. She lives in Santa Barbara, California. To learn more about Daphne, visit her website: www.daphnekingma.com.

Frances Moore Lappé is author or coauthor of sixteen books, including the 1971 best seller *Diet for a Small Planet*. Her most recent book is *Getting a Grip*. She is cofounder of the Institute for Food and Development Policy (Food First) and the Center for Living Democracy, a ten-year initiative to accelerate the spread of democratic innovation. She speaks and writes widely and has received seventeen honorary doctorates as well as the 1987 Right Livelihood Award. You can learn more about Frances by visiting her website: www.smallplanet.org.

Jan Phillips is an award-winning writer, photographer, and multimedia artist. She is the author of *The Art of Original Thinking: The Making of a Thought Leader, Divining the Body, God Is at Eye Level: Photography as a Healing Art, Marry Your Muse, Making Peace,* and *A Waist is a Terrible Thing to Mind.* She has taught in more than twenty-three countries and conducts workshops nationally in creativity, consciousness, and spirituality. You can learn more about Jan by visiting her website: www.janphillips.com.

Joyce Rupp, a recipient of *U.S. Catholic's* national award for furthering the cause of women in the Church, describes herself as a "spiritual midwife." This award-winning author, with more than a million books in print, ministers to women as a spiritual companion, conference speaker, and retreat facilitator. She is a transpersonal psychologist, a member of the Servants of Mary community, and a volunteer for Hospice. To learn more about Joyce, visit her website: www.joycerupp.com.

Michelle Tsosie Sisneros is a Santa Clara/Navajo/Laguna/ Mission Indian artist who lives in Santa Clara Pueblo, New Mexico. The images she paints are inspired by the people who touch her life and Mother Earth. She has won numerous awards and honors for her paintings, including those granted by the Sante Fe Indian Market, the Gallup Ceremonial, and the Sundance Festival. She is the illustrator of the award-winning children's book *Kokopelli's Gift*. You can learn more about Michelle by visiting her website: www.michelletsosiesisneros .com.

Mari Gayatri Stein's insightful words and drawings have delighted readers for more than twenty years. Her books, *Unleashing Your Inner Dog: Your Best Friend's Guide to Life* and *The Buddha Smiles* are stories about love, spirit, and heart doused with humor, irony, and hope. She has recently completed a children's picture book and is the illustrator of *Buddy's Candle* by Dr. Bernie Siegel. She teaches yoga and meditation. To learn more about Mari, visit her website: www.gypsydogpress.com.

Sue Patton Thoele is a psychotherapist and former hospice chaplain. Sue has authored eleven books, including *The Courage to Be Yourself, The Woman's Book of Soul, Growing Hope, Freedoms After 50,* and *The Mindful Woman.* She and her husband, Gene, live in Colorado near their adult children and grandchildren.

Rev. Dr. Iyanla Vanzant travels globally, passionately delivering her special brand of self-empowerment and inspiration to others. As founder and director of Inner Visions Institute of Spiritual Development, Iyanla shares her knowledge of Universal Principle and Law, Eastern and Western spiritual/ religious traditions and teachings, and the truth of unconditional love to motivate others to create a better life, a better community, and a better world. Her newest book is *Tapping* *the Power Within.* To learn more about Iyanla, visit her website: www.innervisionsworldwide.com.

Doreen Virtue, PhD, holds two university degrees in Counseling Psychology from Chapman University in California. A fourth-generation metaphysician and spiritual healer, Doreen has been seeing and talking to angels since early childhood. Doreen writes a weekly column for *Woman's World Magazine* (North America) and a monthly column for *Spirit & Destiny Magazine* (UK). She has appeared on *Oprah, The View,* CNN, and other television and radio programs and hosts a weekly radio show. Doreen's books are published in twenty-six languages. You can learn more about Doreen by visiting her website: www.angeltherapy.com.

The Journey Continues . . .

at www.yourtruestself.com. Continue to explore your personal truths and connect with other women who are embracing their truest selves, just like you! Support is important whenever we are engaged in an inner process as important as this. It is community that can lend a helping hand, offer a listening heart, or a big dose of courage to keep going when we're feeling challenged or weak. Living as your truest self is the work of a lifetime, and there is a community of marvelous women forming to support you every step of the way.

Join me at www.yourtruestself.com to blog your thoughts, gain new insights, or explore new spiritual practices. Participate in teleconferences and networking events. Meet more spiritual luminaries, women who have further insights and truths to share with you for your ongoing journey. Inspiration and support is just a click away. I look forward to meeting you there!

Described by her readers, audiences, and colleagues as "practical and poetic, possessing deep and gentle wisdom," **Janice Lynne Lundy** serves as an interfaith spiritual guide to tens of thousands of women throughout the United States through her nationally syndicated magazine column in *Women's LifeStyle* magazine, and as a professional speaker and retreat facilitator. She has been recognized for her sensitive and compelling interviews as well as for her gift for connecting with soul-searching women. Lundy is an adjunct staff member at the Institute of Spirituality at the Dominican Center at Marywood in Grand Rapids, Michigan. She resides on the peaceful shoreline of Grand Traverse Bay in northern Michigan.

Spirituality for Women

The Circle of Life
The Heart's Journey Through the Seasons
Joyce Rupp and Macrina Wiederkehr
Artwork by Mary Southard
Reflections, poems, prayers, and meditations help us to explore the relationship between the seasons of the earth and the seasons of our lives. *A reflective resource for individuals and groups whose goal is to deepen the inner life. —Presence*
ISBN: 9781893732827 / 288 pages / $19.95

The Star in My Heart
Experiencing Sophia, Inner Wisdom
Joyce Rupp
Joyce Rupp reflects on her personal awakening to the feminine wisdom of Sophia and encourages us to explore Sophia's quiet guidance and come away refreshed.
ISBN: 9781893732834 / 128 pages / $12.95

Loving Yourself More
101 Meditations on Self-Esteem for Women
Virginia Ann Froehle, R.S.M.
This redesigned edition reminds busy women of God's love and offers them an easy way to take the time to love themselves with 101 brief, inspiring meditations. Readers say it "contains down-to-earth, real-life reflections that support my individual journey," and "I find my inner peace reading these words."
ISBN: 9781594711312 / 160 pages / $10.95

Let in the Light
Facing the Hard Stuff with Hope
Patricia H. Livingston
Encourages readers to reframe their response to darkness, to embrace life's imperfections, and let the light stream in.
ISBN: 9781933495002 / 160 pages / $12.95

AmP
ave maria press®

Available from your bookstore or from
ave maria press / Notre Dame, IN 46556
www.avemariapress.com / Ph: 800-282-1865
A Ministry of the Indiana Province of Holy Cross

Keycode: FD9Ø6Ø8ØØØØ